New Labour's
Educational Agenda

THE FUTURE OF EDUCATION FROM 14+

New Labour's Educational Agenda

Issues and Policies for Education and Training from 14+

**Ann Hodgson and
Ken Spours**

**KOGAN
PAGE**

First published 1999

Kogan Page Limited
120 Pentonville Road
London N1 9JN

British Library Cataloguing in Publication Data

A CIP record for this book is available from the British Library.

ISBN 0 7494 2608 X

Typeset by Kogan Page Limited
Printed and bound in Great Britain by Clays Ltd, St Ives plc

Contents

Contents

Acknowledgements

There are many people to whom we are grateful for helping us to write this book.

First of all we would like to thank our families who, once again, have actively supported and encouraged us to complete what has been quite a difficult but rewarding task.

Second, we would like to offer a special thank you to Nick Pearce at IPPR who has been a constant source of support and advice. However, at the end of the day, we take full responsibility for the contents of the book.

Third, thanks are also due to Ministers and officials who kindly gave up their time to be interviewed. They provided us with an invaluable insight into the policy process.

There are a number of people who either commented on early drafts of chapters or provided us with up-to-date sources. We are very grateful to the following for their help: Nadine Cartner, Bert Clough, Dan Finn, Andy Green, Yvonne Hillier, Chris Humphries, Richard Layard, Tom Leney, Geoff Lucas, Norman Lucas, Claus Moser, Michael J Richardson, William Richardson, David Robertson, Peter Robinson, Tom Schuller, John Seymour, Dan Taubman, Alan Tuckett, Martyn Waring, Keith Weller, Alan Wells, Chris Wood, Simon Wood and Michael Young.

Finally, thanks to Wendelien Brada and Jonathan Simpson for their help with the production of the text. We would also like to remember Pat Lomax of Kogan Page, who first suggested the idea for the book over a drink to celebrate the 30th anniversary of Kogan Page. Little did we know what we were taking on! However, it was worth it.

Introduction – Talking About New Labour

Perceptions of New Labour

In May 1997, following New Labour's landslide victory in the general election we were asked whether we would be interested in writing a book on their emerging education and training policies from 14+. At that time, everyone was fascinated by New Labour and how they might change the country after 17 years of Conservative Government. There was a strong feeling of expectation about what the new Government might do, particularly in relation to education, because of its central importance to New Labour's overall mission, summed up in Tony Blair's famous phrase, 'education, education, education'.

Two years on, people are still fascinated by New Labour, but they do not know quite what to make of it. Now that the Government's extended honeymoon period is over, people are asking about the precise nature of its strategy for education and training. We will argue that there are basically two reasons for people's enduring interest and mounting confusion.

First, there is the whole issue of the 'Third Way', what it is, what it means and how it is translated into policy. In the book, we attempt to provide a way of addressing these questions and looking at what the Third Way means in relation to policy for education and training from 14+. It has been suggested that the Third Way can be seen as a position which lies between the 'dynamism of flexible markets of North America and the social regulation and inclusivity of Continental social democratic models' (Hillman, 1998: 65). We suggest that the Third Way can also be seen as a pragmatic response to the historical legacies of both the Conservative's marketized era and the Labour Party's past corporatism and 'tax and spend' image. The former interpretation suggests a fundamentally new political position – hence 'New' Labour. The latter characterizes New Labour's Third Way approach as largely reactive to its own national constraints and, therefore, with the passage of time, it could evolve in a new direction. From the evidence that we have collected for this book, we suggest that any concept of the Third Way in relation to education and training policy from 14+ is based more on the latter than on the former.

The second reason why it is difficult to provide an overall picture of New Labour's approach to education is because of its different emphases in the compulsory and the post-compulsory phases. Despite the common themes of standards and investing more in education, we argue in this book that New Labour has taken quite different approaches to compulsory and post-compulsory education and training.

New Labour's approach to compulsory education is dominated by the desire to raise educational standards by centralized initiatives and regulatory systems. These include: greater central control over school management, curriculum and teaching methods; the use of agencies such as Ofsted to challenge the teaching profession and education research; the focus on literacy and numeracy; the emphasis on traditional methods of assessment and pedagogy; the introduction of specialist provision for different types of learners; increased parental responsibility for children's attendance, behaviour and achievement; and an encouragement of public–private partnerships. The desire to bring about change quickly has led to a tough accountability-driven approach to providers which brooks no opposition and has led to considerable antagonism from the teaching profession.

In contrast to this assertive, centralized approach to compulsory education, New Labour's approach to post-compulsory education and training is much more cautious, experimental and voluntarist. Although in certain areas, such as the New Deal, there is an element of compulsion and regulation, for the most part, New Labour has continued to follow the previous administration's permissive or voluntarist approach.

This difference of approach to compulsory and post-compulsory education and training is partly the result of the latter being seen as of a second order in terms of policy hierarchy and also because of the complex set of issues involved which span education, training and the labour market. The problems of compulsory education had to be resolved quickly to create a springboard for the future. On the other hand, post-compulsory education and training (the 18–24 New Deal excepted) is seen as something which can evolve more slowly over time. This is one of the reasons why our discussion of strategy focuses on an agenda for a second term of office rather than on immediate reform.

Explicit and planned change rather than policy evolution

Throughout the book we argue that New Labour's policies in relation to education and training from 14+ have been largely dominated by responses to the Conservative legacy, although there are different emphases in New Labour's overall approach, notably their focus on social and educational inclusion.

We characterize their reaction to the Conservative legacy, and in particular, their attempts to modify the effects of marketization as a Third Way 'weak framework' approach. We contrast this approach with what we describe in our final chapter as a Third Way 'strong framework' approach to education and training from 14+. What we argue throughout the book is that a weak framework approach relies heavily on voluntarist and initiatives-led reform which does not adequately address deep-seated divisions and barriers within the education and training system. Moreover, we suggest that this approach is likely to be frustrated by the system barriers which New Labour appears to be reluctant to address during this Parliament.

Another feature of the Third Way weak framework approach from 14+ is that it relies on evolutionary policy change which, at its most extreme, is actively shaped by pressures from both Right and Left. This approach means that it is difficult for people to understand the future direction of policy. This may have short-term political advantages, but it does not adequately engage people or prepare them for longer-term change. In the final analysis, this tacit evolutionary approach to policy is less than democratic, because it tends to rely on working behind the scenes and second guessing policy decisions. In arguing for a strong framework approach, what we, therefore, advocate is gradual and planned change with an explicit end point, so that people know where they are going, can prepare for reform and can actively engage in the reform process.

Why we agreed to write this book

Surveying and assessing New Labour's approach to education and training from 14+ has not been easy. It is always difficult capturing and analysing policy as it happens, because you do not have the benefit of hindsight. This is particularly the case with a new government which claims that it has a 'new' and evolving policy approach. The book, therefore, aims to provide a comprehensive picture of emerging policies and issues at this particular time, although we hope that its underlying analysis may be more enduring.

It has even been difficult to decide on how to structure the account of New Labour's policies for education and training from 14+. Eventually, as you will see, we decided on the major themes of lifelong learning, the New Deal, skills, training and the world of work, the reform of further and higher education and qualifications and curriculum from 14+. Rightly or wrongly, we decided not to have a discrete chapter on the theme of disaffection and social exclusion, despite its central role in New Labour's thinking. Due to its pervasiveness, this theme has been covered as an integral part of all chapters.

Interviews with ministers, policy advisers and civil servants have helped us to texture what we have written, although we have not been able to quote them directly. Apart from being useful as a means of research, the opportunity to talk with those directly involved with the policy process has given us an insight into the difficulties of being in government as opposed to being in opposition. Glimpsing the realities of government has served to reinforce our commitment, expressed in past work, to the idea of a gradual approach to change combined with open debate and a strong vision of the future.

Writing this book has further strengthened our desire to contribute to an open debate about the future of education and training from 14+. The book aims, ambitiously, to engage with the concerns of the different constituencies involved in educational research, policy and practice. This is the concept that lies behind our Kogan Page series on *The Future of Education from 14+*. We hope, therefore, that this first book in the series will be of use to education practitioners, policy-makers and those in the research community.

1

New Labour, the 'Third Way' and Post-compulsory Education and Training

Education is the key to economic success, social cohesion and active citizenship. Our future national prosperity depends on the skills and abilities of our people. In a rapidly changing, technologically advanced and increasingly competitive global economy, Britain needs a world-class system of education and training. The regular updating of skills and knowledge has become essential to maintaining and enhancing productivity and security in the workplace.

(Labour Party, 1996a: 2).

Introduction

Education, or more accurately, lifelong learning, has become central to the political philosophy, economic strategy and social policy of the Labour Party. This is not just a matter of establishing a hierarchy of policy objectives in which education becomes the 'passion' of the government; it is also about the response of political parties and policymakers to far-reaching socio-economic changes in advanced capitalist societies. Globalization of the economy, increasingly rapid technological change and the transformation of labour markets have made education and training central instruments of economic and social policymaking. For New Labour, lifelong learning is seen to be the key to the development of an inclusive and just society whose economy is successfully competitive in the global market-place. In this chapter, we therefore set out to explore New Labour's approach to 14+ education and training within the broader contexts both of economic policy-making and globalization.[1]

New Labour, globalization and education and training

Broadly speaking, globalization refers to trends in the global economy – the internationalization of production, increased capital flows and the growth of world markets in goods and services – which are held to be unprecedented in magnitude and consequence for nation states, national economies, politics and for education (Reich, 1991; Miliband, 1994). Theorists of globalization cite vast increases in foreign direct investment and overseas trade, the growth of transnational corporations, and, most critically, the spectacular development of international finance markets, as overwhelming evidence for a 'qualitative shift in the nature of economic activity' (Perraton, 1997: 226). This shift has been seen as fundamentally redrawing political, social and cultural boundaries.

They see education and training now directly as the objects, rather than the adjuncts, of economic policy. In large part, this is a consequence of the collapse of the post-war Keynesian economic consensus. Over the last two decades, governments in advanced capitalist democracies have steadily abandoned so-called Keynesian economic strategies (Corrie, 1997). The arrival of 'stagflation' in the 1960s and 1970s – when growth slowed, unemployment rose, but inflation also increased sharply – directly challenged key tenets of mainstream economic thinking of the time. During the 1980s, the confidence of the Left in radical macro-economic policies waned considerably. Expansionary demand management gave way to reliance on the now prevalent orthodoxies of macro-economic policy: the pursuit of low inflation, secure public finances and long-term stability in the economic environment (Corrie, 1997; Elliott, 1998). With this shift away from active demand-management, the policy focus has switched to supply-side measures, most particularly education and training policies.

Rethinking of economic policy on the Left was also a recognition of wider changes in the socio-economic landscape. The Keynesian approach rested upon central pillars or 'organizational premises' (Rogers and Streeck, 1994: 30) which have been substantially undermined or eroded in the past two decades: central direction over economic policy and activity by the nation state; capital dominated by large firms; and an organized labour movement structured by the Fordist production paradigm.[2] Giddens (1998: 16) summarizes the social foundations of 'old' social democracy as follows:

- a social system and a traditional family form which permitted an unambiguous male breadwinner definition of full employment;
- an homogeneous labour market in which men threatened with unemployment were mostly manual workers;
- the dominance of mass production in basic sectors of the economy which created stable, if unrewarding, conditions of work for many in the labour force;
- an elitist state staffed by small groups of public-spirited experts;

- national economies that were substantially contained within sovereign boundaries, since Keynesianism presumed the preponderance of the domestic economy over external trade in goods and services.

Reich (1991) suggests that in the political discourse of contemporary social democracy, globalization of the economy, technological change and social shifts have swept away these structural and social foundations of the post-war Keynesian consensus. In its place, according to Brown, Blunkett and Harman (1996), is a less certain, more competitive but ultimately more dynamic world economy, in which any country's prosperity depends above all else on the skills, knowledge and inventiveness of its people.

A common interpretation of this context is that the process of globalization draws to a close the era of 'big government' in which nation states had the power to intervene in economic activity and to make significant choices over the direction of economic and social policy. According to this particular rendition of the 'end of history' thesis, nation states are now so constrained by global markets and the power of footloose transnational corporations that political differences at the national level largely disappear (Reich, 1991). However, such claims for economic globalization and its consequences remain hotly contested.

The dominant interpretation of globalization in the 1980s was neo-liberal. Governments of the neo-liberal New Right sought to reduce the economic management role of government, to privatize public sector activities and to produce an ideal of the low-taxation, low-spending and *laissez-faire* state (Elliott, 1998). However, nearly 20 years of neo-liberal experimentation, particularly in the United States and the UK, have exposed serious economic and social dysfunctions – notably social polarization and the running down of social infrastructures and, in the case of the UK, 'boom and bust' approaches to economic management. By the early 1990s, the intellectual and political hegemony of neo-liberalism began to wane (Hutton, 1995).

A second strand of analysis is sceptical about the whole concept of globalization and the way in which it has been used in such a sweeping manner. This perspective sees globalization as an economic phenomenon which is more uneven and conjunctural than has been claimed by more extreme globalization theorists (Hirst and Thompson, 1996; Weiss, 1997). Moreover, it can be argued that while neo-liberal ideas of economic management have generally held sway over the last two decades, they have been developed as more complete political and state strategies in only a minority of countries. Most continental European countries have developed a different response to globalization, in which popular pressure has led the state to play a more regulatory role in the economy, without a large-scale dismantling of social welfare structures (Green, 1997). This has been termed the 'social capitalist' model and is reflected in social and economic policies in the Nordic countries, by the Christian Democrats in Germany and governments of different political persuasions in France (Hutton, 1995). The Germans and French, in particular, have tried to forge a transnational economic model based on the European Union and accompanied by a strong social agenda. The countries of the Pacific Rim have also followed a more state-led regulatory path, though with more authoritarian regimes and a social agenda aimed at nation building (Green, 1997).

New Labour and the Third Way

Beyond these two tendencies – a neo-liberal model and a social capitalist model – another strand of thinking known as the 'Third Way' has emerged, which is forming itself into an ideological bedrock of the Blair, and arguably, the Clinton administrations. In the New Labour theoretical framework, globalization constrains the power of nation states over economic policy so that there can be no return to 'go-it-alone' demand management or dashes for growth. At the same time, however, such an understanding opens up a new enabling role for government: one in which investment in skills and infrastructure equips people and businesses to thrive in the competitive economic environment created by globalization (Blair, 1999).

New Labour has now sought to articulate this theoretical perspective as a Third Way for 21st century centre-left politics, seeing it as a position which lies somewhere between continental European and American models of both the economy and the state (Hillman, 1998). The strategic goal is to find a means of reconciling social democratic and European values of social justice, decency and inclusion with the employment-orientated, flexible labour markets of the United States. The concept of a Third Way is an emerging powerful paradigm in New Labour thinking which, arguably, fundamentally affects its commitment to supply-side strategies such as education and training.

Like the concept of globalization, the concept of the Third Way is also contested and subject to different interpretations. It can be seen as a middle position between the neo-liberal model and the state socialist model – in this sense it can be seen as a form of market socialism (Giddens, 1994) or as a renewed social democracy (Giddens, 1998). New Labour, however, appears to have cast it more narrowly (or more to the Right than this) as a middle way between neo-liberal models and social capitalist models of the role of the State. The concept of the Third Way is, therefore, a contested concept and a focus of debate within New Labour as well as more widely (White, 1998). In the final chapter of this book, we will take forward this notion by suggesting that the Third Way concept in relation to post-14 education and training can be seen to have two possible variants – 'weak' and 'strong' frameworks – reflecting different emphases on the role of the State.

New Labour, the Third Way and the role of the State

New Labour's response to globalization, emphasizing the limits of macro-economic management and linked to the Reichian argument about the primacy of knowledge and skills, has provided a strong conceptual rationale for the reform of the welfare state. Despite its neo-liberal commitment to a minimal State, its role actually grew under 18 years of Conservative government, not least because of the increasing need for welfare support to tackle the problems caused by unemployment and recession. Between 1979 and 1996, a total of £43 billion was spent on social security, yet poverty increased and society became more unequal (DSS, 1997).

New Labour subscribes to a notion of a modernized or 'enabling' State (Blair, 1996). This too can be taken as evidence of a Third Way between a Keynesian administrative State and a neo-liberal minimal State. Central to New Labour's vision of building a dynamic economy is keeping taxes low and public expenditure under control in order to provide the best environment for private investment, while investing proportionately more of the public purse in health, education and, possibly, transport. The assumption is that financial stability and steady growth will, over the economic cycle, provide sufficient revenue to finance these services. For this to happen, it would be necessary to restructure the welfare state and to shift the unemployed from welfare to work, so that they move from absorbing public expenditure to contributing to taxes. New Labour sees this process not only as an economic imperative, but also as the basis of creating greater social cohesion.

This conceptual framework for public service provision has been termed the 'social investment State' (Giddens, 1998: 117). Giddens argues that we need a new understanding of the role of the State: 'The guideline is investment in human capital wherever possible, rather than direct provision of economic maintenance. In place of the welfare state we should put the social investment State, operating in the context of a positive welfare [ie individual well-being] society.'

The social investment State of the Third Way seeks to invest in human capability through lifelong learning; to build new partnerships between the public and private sectors to maximize the most effective contribution of each; to draw individuals, government and the voluntary and private sectors into new relationships of mutual support and responsibility; and to strengthen families as the bedrock of social stability.

The importance of lifelong learning for New Labour's Third Way approach

The centrality of education and training to employment and employability has also brought lifelong learning more sharply into focus within the Labour

Government's political philosophy (see Chapter 2). New Labour argues that investment in knowledge and skills will provide the essential foundation of both individual employability and the competitiveness of an economy based on high value-added goods and services which are tradable in the global market-place. Second, labour market flexibility will ensure that the British economy can create jobs on a sufficient scale to tackle social exclusion. Finally, reform of the welfare state is necessary to ensure that welfare provision becomes a springboard back into work rather than a safety net generating 'dependency' and reinforcing social exclusion (Labour Party, 1995a).

Like the concepts of globalization and the Third Way, the primacy of education and training as a political strategy is also contested. It has been seen by some simply as rhetoric and electoral pragmatism, since education pays dividends both nationally and personally and education and training reform is less contentious than employment and fiscal policies (Avis *et al*, 1996). However, the extent of New Labour's recent policy debates on economic and political changes suggest that there is both a deep-seated commitment to education and training which, at the same time, is reinforced by the perception of possible electoral advantage.

New Labour is still reaching towards a coherent political philosophy. In sketch, however, its elements are clear, and learning occupies a central part (DfEE, 1998a). New Labour, in common with political parties across the developed world, has entered a period of governance driven by the recognition that skills, knowledge and intellectual capital are now critical determinants of individual life chances and of the relationships between individuals, their employers and the wider society of which they are a part. As such, learning must underpin any contemporary egalitarian philosophy.

Education has always been central to the political philosophy of the Left, both as a means of emancipation in itself and as an arena of public policy action which is fundamental to egalitarian strategies. But learning is now more important to concepts of social justice than ever before. As the demand for extended education and training has grown, disadvantage or exclusion in the labour market and wider society suffered by those lacking basic literacy and numeracy skills has hardened. Moreover, this marginalization is compounded as people get older (Bynner and Parsons, 1997). Without recurrent opportunities to tackle basic skills deficits and to improve educational attainment, those with poor levels of literacy and numeracy are likely to face increased social exclusion.

In an effort to address the political philosophy of the Labour Party to these realities of contemporary patterns of social exclusion, Gordon Brown sought to elaborate a 'maximalist' concept of equality of opportunity (Brown, 1996). Rejecting so-called 'equality of outcome' as socially undesirable and politically untenable, Brown promoted an expansive notion of equality of opportunity which seeks to tackle widening inequality and social exclusion through a series of government interventions. Foremost amongst these is the use of education and training to improve individuals' access to the labour market and to enhance their job security. Rather than alleviate poverty and reduce income differentials through increased taxation and redistributive welfare spending, Brown argued that the most effective means of tackling inequality and social exclusion was to provide recurrent equality of opportunity for individuals to learn and earn throughout their working lives. Brown's approach to equality of opportunity is based on life-long learning, a reformed welfare state and mutuality at a local level. Persistent or concentrated labour market exclusion and disadvantage, and hence structural inequalities will, therefore, be limited.

So far, we have demonstrated how New Labour's approach to education and training has been shaped by its responses to globalization and its view of the role of the State in economic and social policy. However, we will argue that its Third Way approach to post-compulsory education and training has also been fundamentally influenced by its response to the Conservative legacy.

The Conservative legacy

The Conservative legacy can be seen to consist of two dimensions: first, political and ideological assumptions which built up over the 17 years of government about issues such as public administration, markets and education standards and second, the structure and funding of education and training.

The Conservative political and ideological legacy

Over their three terms in office, successive Conservative governments were very active in the area of post-compulsory education and training with a series of programmes, initiatives and White Papers. Throughout this period, a Conservative paradigm for delivering public services emerged which was based on privatizing a range of public services, promoting market competition, diminishing the role of public administration and creating quangos to provide funding steers. This market approach was first applied to compulsory education through local management of schools and opting out at the end of the 1980s and then spread to post-compulsory education in the early 1990s. The 1991 White Paper *Education and Training for the 21st Century* (DES/ED/WO, 1991) and the FHE Act (1992) heralded a high water mark for market-oriented approaches to education and training.

In assessing New Labour's approach to creating its own political agenda in the late 1990s, it is worth remembering that the Conservative market paradigm had, in fact, taken over a decade to emerge. It was only making a major impact by the early 1990s with incorporation of further education colleges, training credits, outcome-related funding and outcome-based awards such as National Vocational Qualifications (NVQs).

By the mid-1990s, however, the limitations of these approaches were becoming apparent. Training credits pilots demonstrated that this approach did not increase motivation or choice for 16–19-year-olds (Hodkinson and Sparkes, 1994); TECs became the deliverers of government policies on adult unemployment and failed to increase substantially employers' involvement in education and training (Robinson, 1996); the new qualifications (NVQs and GNVQs) were regularly subjected to criticism from both Left and Right (Senker, 1996) and the newly-incorporated further education sector reached a state of financial crisis (Spours and Lucas, 1996).

By the mid-1990s, Conservative education policy entered a more pragmatic or consolidatory phase of policy as the prevailing political tide precluded more radical market-oriented approaches. Modern Apprenticeships were introduced in 1994 in response to the rapid decline of apprenticeships and there were reviews of 16–19 qualifications (Dearing, 1996); of higher education (NCIHE, 1997) and of further education (Kennedy, 1997). These adjustments and their implementation processes formed an important part of the Conservative legacy for New Labour.

New Labour thus inherited an education and training state which, up until the general election, was still going through a process of 'consolidation and review'. This 'pragmatic' phase of the Conservative legacy meant that both structures and policy initiatives related to the education and training system could be steered in different directions – there was no set course. It also meant that New Labour's approach to post-compulsory education and training shows more lines of continuity with the late phase of the Conservative administration than had been apparent in much of the pre-election rhetoric.

In the two years prior to the general election, New Labour's response to education and training policy was to attack the Conservative Government on the grounds of lack of structural coherence in the system, the variability of examination standards, the negative effects of institutional competition on cost-effective partnerships and student choice; the inequalities affecting student participation; the lack of democratic accountability and poor system performance (Labour Party, 1996a). Furthermore, New Labour committed itself to creating 'a framework for developing a modern, flexible, fair and efficient structure of post-compulsory education for both individuals and institutions' (Labour Party, 1996a: 2).

While the Conservative ideological paradigm had reached its limits by the mid-1990s, it nevertheless left a marked impression on New Labour in two major respects. First, New Labour, determined not be saddled with an Old Labour 'tax and spend' image, adhered to the Conservative's public spending limits for the first two years of office. In practical terms, this meant an initial unpopular delay in spending on education, particularly in the post-compulsory sector, although there is now the promise of generous funding for further and higher education, particularly in relation to widening participation. However, New Labour's 'prudence' in its first two years of office may have framed education ministers' attitudes towards reform measures. For example, there is a strong emphasis on voluntarism and individual responsibility in *The Learning Age* Green Paper (DfEE, 1998a), which will be examined in detail in Chapter 2.

A second powerful ideological legacy has been the issue of standards in compulsory and post-compulsory education. New Labour is committed to improving literacy standards in schools and making examination standards more consistent in post-compulsory education, while, at the same time, broadening the post-16 curriculum and widening participation in education and training. As Chapter 6 argues, this may end up producing tensions between maintaining A level standards and increasing achievement by way of a more flexible curriculum and qualifications framework.

The education and training system legacy

The Conservatives left New Labour with an education and training system which in terms of participation and achievement had doubled its outputs over 17 years. By the mid-1990s, however, system growth, at least for initial post-compulsory education, was also showing distinct signs of running out of steam (Spours, 1998).

In retrospect, the Conservatives can be seen to have enjoyed four successes in terms of education and training system performance. In the early 1980s, they provided low-level education and training for large sections of the cohort as an alternative to youth unemployment. This was followed in the late 1980s by a largely unplanned and demand-led expansion of full-time education participation in schools, colleges and in higher education. During this period, achievement rates rose from a low baseline, though these were largely confined to the two upper quartiles of the 14–19 age group. Moreover, participation increases were realized at lower unit costs in further education and in work-based training, though not in school sixth forms (Richardson *et al*, 1995).

However, these successes masked system weaknesses. While the overall national position improved, the UK did not succeed in catching up with other European countries and was overtaken by those on the Pacific Rim in terms of full-time participation rates, basic skills and examination achievement (Steedman and Green, 1997). New Labour, therefore, faces a legacy in which improvements through voluntarist approaches have plateaued and a growing minority has been excluded from success.

This presents a dilemma for New Labour, because it cannot simply go with the flow of strong growth trends in the education and training system, with the exception possibly of sections of the work-based route such as Modern Apprenticeships. Instead, the new Government has to decide how to tackle an education and training system which has excluded large sections of youth and which, in the mid-1990s, is not expanding. Each of the subsequent chapters in this book examines how New Labour is attempting to address this issue in different aspects of its education and training policy from 14+.

Old Labour and New Labour on education and training

How the Government will tackle these problems can be further illustrated by the 'distance' Labour has travelled in terms of its approach to policy over the last two decades. The aim of this section of the chapter is to outline the main trends in Labour's past thinking about post-compulsory education and training and to assess how far New Labour is building upon, or is breaking with, these historical trends.

Period 1 (1964–70): The white-hot heat of the technological revolution

Recent history of Labour policy in post-compulsory education is seen to date from its election victory in 1964. Labour's 'New Britain' manifesto with its emphasis on modernization through the 'white-hot technological revolution' saw a reliance on central manpower planning, the genesis of the Manpower Services Commission (MSC), the rise of the Industrial Training Boards (ITBs) and the rapid expansion of higher education (McCarthy, 1997). It was essentially a Keynesian or Fordist approach to economic management which was then reflected in education and training.

Period 2 (1974–79): The crisis of confidence in the post-war model

Labour in Government in the 1970s saw a continuation of a faith in central state management of employment, modelled on the Swedish Labour Market Board (Ainley and Corney, 1990) with the MSC publishing its 'Comprehensive Manpower Planning' (McCarthy, 1997). At the same time, the Labour Government, under pressure from the aftermath of the oil crisis, suffered a crisis of confidence in the ability of liberal education to meet the needs of the economy (Hargreaves, 1989). The defining moment was James Callaghan's Ruskin speech in 1976 in which he argued for what McCarthy terms 'non-elitist vocationalism' (Callaghan, 1976). The remainder of the Labour Parliament was focused on the role of the MSC, and the development of job creation schemes, notably the Youth Opportunities Programme (YOP), in response to rising youth unemployment.

Period 3 (the mid-1980s): Labour's left turn

In Opposition, Labour took a political turn to the Left which was mirrored in post-compulsory education and training policy and debates. Party thinking during this period was reflected in a document *Education and Training: Options for Labour* (Labour Party, 1986). It could best be described as a radical and socialist approach with a stress on planning and democracy at both national and local level. There was an accent on local authority planning agreements, worker co-operatives and public enterprise, and, at a national level, arguments for a department of education and training with a unified national and local delivery system.

The document argued, however, that Labour should not try to return to a 'golden age' of apprenticeship, that the education and training system had been elitist and that the ITBs were not able to work in a cross-sectoral way. The document was both a critique of the policies of the Conservative Government and an attempt to create an approach based on a democratized national and local state. It was written at the level of political principles rather than practical strategies. Its 'oppositionalist' tone and lack of practical coherence reflected what McCaig (1997) has described as Labour's 'producer-capture' approach of the mid-1980s which made its policies and debates vulnerable to interest group lobbying.

Period 4 (early 1990s): Emerging consensus on frameworks to empower individuals

By the early 1990s, Labour debates were fast evolving and outlined themes which were to be elaborated more fully in the Blair era. This was not only due to the way that both Neil Kinnock and John Smith modernized the Labour Party to make it more electable, but was also the result of an emerging professional consensus in the area. By the early 1990s, the Labour Party was turning outwards and making more use of specialist advice from a range of sources and not just political and trade union groups (McCaig, 1997). This keyed Labour into a growing professional consensus on the need for both the unification of the qualifications system and for a more individualist and consumer-oriented approach to learning and achievement. *Opening Doors* (Labour Party, 1992a), with its stress on a unified qualifications system, access, partnership and empowering individuals in a learning society was a forerunner of New Labour's approach which was to emerge more fully following Tony Blair's election as Labour leader. The Left, however, saw this document as a revisiting of 'the Wilsonian rhetoric of the "white-hot heat of the technological revolution" recycled in post-Fordist terms' (Hatcher, 1994).

Period 5 (1993–96): The emergence of New Labour's new agenda

The three years prior to the 1997 general election saw a wave of innovation in New Labour's educational thinking revolving around the political relationship of Blair, Brown, Harman and Blunkett. This period could rightly be termed the emergence of New Labour's new agenda for education and training. The Labour Party published a range of policy documents on post-compulsory education and training including *University for Industry*

(1994), *Labour's New Deal for Britain's under 25s* (1995b), *A New Economic Future for Britain* (1995a), *Lifelong Learning* (1996a), *Aiming Higher* (1996b), *Equipping Young People for the Future: From welfare to education* (1996c) and *Learn as You Earn: Labour's plans for a skills revolution* (1996d), which outlined Labour's macro-economic approach. These documents provided the framework of thinking which Labour carried into government in 1997. Taken together, they represented a far more comprehensive approach than previous documents by connecting macro-economic policy, the reform of the welfare state, qualifications reform, training and the work-based route and lifelong learning.

Period 6: (1997–98) New Labour in government: political focus and constraint

The first 18 months of New Labour in government can be seen as a period in which the new administration focused on manifesto commitments, gave an absolute priority to welfare to work and was influenced by the impact of a range of constraints. McCaig (1997) argues that since 1994, New Labour has faced a series of related constraints – electoral, economic, ideological and institutional.

Since the election, the inter-relationship of constraints has become even more prominent and powerful – adherence to Conservative spending limits in the first two years, a focus on specific manifesto commitments (rather than the wider agenda of pre-election policy documents), a determination not to alienate sections of the voting population (reflected by a concern about how policies will be perceived and described by sections of the press) and the endemic problem of how to turn policy themes into practical strategies.

It is also becoming clear that New Labour in government has developed a hierarchy of political objectives in education and training. In post-compulsory education four themes have come to politically dominate in the first 18 months – guarding education standards, tackling long-term unemployment through the New Deal, focusing on basic skills and widening participation in education and training. All four are central to the political strategy of pursuing educational and social inclusion, of keeping ideologically in touch with middle England and, at the same time, ensuring that the social security budget is reduced, thereby releasing more funds for investment in health and education.

Currently, New Labour appears to have left behind much of its historical thinking in relation to education and training from 14+. By the early 1990s, it was beginning to embrace themes on individual responsibility and accountability which mirrored the ideology of the Conservatives. At the same time, however, New Labour began to build a distinctive and comprehensive supply-side approach which emphasized the enabling role of the State through qualifications frameworks and training programmes allied to welfare and funding reform. Nevertheless, the Old Labour legacy persists, albeit reflected in background arguments. In the past, Labour has argued for greater state regulation in relation to the demand for skills and the labour market, for a more democratic and accountable infrastructure and investment in local collaboration and institutional partnership. These ideas, we will argue, as part of a 'strong framework' approach may become more relevant in the future as New Labour attempts to move away from having to address the Conservative legacy and, instead, begins to creates the conditions to successfully implement its own policies (see Chapter 7).

New Labour's emerging policy framework (1993–1998)

The aim of this section of the chapter is to briefly locate the major aspects of New Labour's policy framework, to identify the initial problems which have appeared in government and the kind of challenges which will have to be faced in the future if New Labour's policies are to be successful. Each aspect of the framework is pursued in greater depth in each of the subsequent thematic chapters of the book.

The effects of fundamental economic and labour market changes, together with New Labour's egalitarian anti-poverty agenda, suggested that this administration would embark on a radical education and training strategy. So far its radicalism could best be described as 'Radical Centre' rather than 'Radical Centre-left' and consists of three main strands:

- a 'traditionalist interventionist' approach to school standards, marked by an emphasis on basic skills, an eschewing of progressivist learning methods and a private/public approach to certain areas, such as education action zones;
- a 'voluntarist framework partnership' approach to lifelong learning which emphasizes individual responsibility, the use of information technologies and the possible development of a system of units and credits to recognize a wider range of knowledge and skills;
- an 'egalitarian approach' to social and educational inclusion which aims to focus funding on the most marginal groups and to redistribute it towards further education in order to widen participation in education and training.

Below we illustrate briefly how these strands affect New Labour's education and training policy in five major areas which are the focus of the thematic chapters – lifelong learning, welfare to work, learning in the workplace, further and higher education and qualifications and curriculum reform from 14+.

Lifelong learning

Lifelong learning, which is considered in Chapter 2 of this book, is the 'organizing theme' of New Labour's education and training agenda. As a long-term approach, it emerges from the globalization analysis and the argument that education and learning is important across the lifespan, not only for economic competitiveness but also for social cohesion, democracy and personal fulfilment.

New Labour's approach was initially outlined in its pre-election consultation document *Lifelong Learning* (Labour Party, 1996a). This document tried to pull together discussion of a number of emerging strands of Labour policy – Target 2000, welfare to work, reform proposals for further education, initiatives in adult and continuing education, the funding and reform of higher education, work-based education and training, Individual Learning Accounts (ILAs) and the University for Industry (UfI).

New Labour's Green Paper, *The Learning Age* (DfEE, 1998a), attempts to bring together these often quite disparate strands into an overall strategy for lifelong learning. Chapter 2 assesses to what extent this policy document tackles some of the significant barriers to building a coherent, accessible, transparent and attractive lifelong learning system in this country.

Welfare to Work, New Deal and social and educational inclusion

Welfare to Work, which is discussed in some detail in Chapter 3, is New Labour's flagship programme of the current Parliament in relation to post-compulsory education and training. Announced in 1995 as part of Labour's shadow budget, the Welfare to Work approach has given rise to a number of New Deal initiatives. The importance of Welfare to Work lies in the way in which it articulates New Labour's social and educational inclusion agenda. It reflects the expenditure pressures to get the unemployed and particularly young people off benefit and into work. It also fits in with the move for wider reform of the welfare state. This one initiative provides a good example of how New Labour is approaching social policy through collaboration across a number of government departments, but with the Treasury and the Chancellor as driving forces.

Modernizing learning in the workplace

The theme of developing the work-based route and promoting learning in the workplace is embraced by New Labour under its policies for lifelong learning and its macro-economic approaches. Within this book, however, we have decided to treat work-based learning for young people as a distinct theme (though related to the discussion of lifelong learning) not least because of the relative neglect of the work-based route by education and training reformers in the 1990s. Chapter 4, therefore, covers such issues as the training of young people through National Traineeships and Modern Apprenticeships, the role of NVQs and related vocational qualifications and work-based initiatives for adults.

New Labour's approach to learning in the workplace could broadly be described as a 'voluntarist framework and partnership approach'. This involves exhorting employers to offer training and to focus on human resource development, while putting into place a weak framework for partnership and resourcing a number of key initiatives (eg IiP, UfI, ILAs) to support work-based learning.

Reforming further and higher education

Although in New Labour's post-compulsory education and training policy concept the workplace has an increasing role to play in training and skills development, further and higher education are still seen as the main vehicles for realizing the lifelong learning project. A discussion of the role that these two sectors, singly and in tandem, play in the policy process thus forms the focus of Chapter 5 of this book.

Following the general election, two major reports were published on further and higher education – the Kennedy Report *Learning Works: Widening participation in FE* (Kennedy, 1997) and the Dearing Report *Higher Education in the Learning Society* (NCIHE, 1997). Although commissioned by the previous government, these reports were published under New Labour and their findings and recommendations are now very much part of political debate and policy development.

Funding has been the immediate focus of attention in both sectors (despite the fact that both reports included other substantial themes) and significant attempts have already been made to tackle both financial instability and inequalities. The theme of funding widening participation in education and training is also high on the political agenda for both sectors and is likely to remain so because of New Labour's emphasis on equality of access to educational opportunities as a way of addressing social exclusion. Beyond this, the Government has indicated that in the future it wishes to see the development of a regional framework for further education, which would involve the reform of the FEFC, and a focus on quality in the higher education sector.

Curriculum and qualifications reform from 14+

Prior to the election, New Labour emphasized the need for a 'high standard and flexible post-16 curriculum with a long-term objective of developing a coherent and integrated 14–19+ curriculum' (Labour Party, 1996b). Its discussion document, *Aiming Higher* (1996b), argued that a quantum leap in standards and attainment levels was required and that existing qualifications were either too narrow or too bureaucratic to support these objectives.

Once in government, New Labour halted implementation work on the Dearing Report on qualifications reform (Dearing, 1996) and announced the beginning of a further period of consultation which began with the document *Qualifying for Success* (DfEE, 1997a) and culminated in advice from QCA to Ministers in March 1998 when a series of incremental changes to the qualifications system were outlined.

The Government's approach emerging from *Qualifying for Success* has been to stick closely to its limited manifesto commitments; broadening A levels, up-grading vocational qualifications and introducing key skills within a rigorous framework (Labour Party, 1997) rather than immediately to pursue the more radical agenda set out in the latter part of *Aiming Higher*. Chapter 6 discusses this issue in more detail.

Five challenges in post-compulsory education and training facing New Labour

It is becoming clear that New Labour now faces several related challenges in relation to its policies for education and training from 14+. These are concerned with the poor performance of the education and training system as a whole and the need to demonstrate early success in their flagship policies.

System performance

It is going to be far harder for New Labour to achieve measurable success in terms of post-16 participation and achievement than it was for the Conservatives. It was apparent that, by 1995, the previous government had reached the limits of expansion through voluntary participation and through the reduction of unit costs. Retention rates in many post-16 courses were low and many learners remained excluded. Reaching national or international achievement targets with a 'harder to get' sections of the cohort, particularly 16–25 years, will be difficult without a great deal of new investment and co-ordinated effort. The Government will need to both further expand participation in the system and to make participation more efficient, not only in full-time education but also in the work-based route. This is likely to require some radical reforms which involve more structural change than New Labour is currently prepared to consider.

Fulfilling manifesto commitments and succeeding with early priorities

A second challenge is the need for early success in the flagship programmes of New Deal and UfI and to see progress on the central and organizing theme of lifelong learning. A key measure of success will be whether the transition from welfare to work is based on the unemployed, and particularly the young unemployed, achieving real jobs through better skills or whether the New Deal ends up being just another training scheme. The UfI project will need to prove that it has a central role to play in stimulating demand for lifelong learning.

The lifelong learning goal, on the other hand, will be dependent on policy formation across different areas of government and the State due to the interconnection of education, welfare, economic policy and public expenditure strategies. If New Labour's approach to lifelong learning is to work in the longer term, the Government has to shift the UK system from front-loaded to lifelong; from selective and hierarchical to universal and inclusive; and from institution-based to mixed forms of delivery.

Restructuring the education and training State

It follows, therefore, that a third challenge – a medium-term one – is to restructure the education and training system through what we will term a system of 'strong frameworks' (see Chapter 7). The goal of encouraging lifelong learning is going to require greater regional and local planning structures; high quality work-based programmes with a more active contribution from employers and trade unions; a radically reformed 14+ qualifications system; more equitable institutional funding arrangements; new patterns of institutional co-operation and new approaches to pedagogy and financial incentives for individual learners. This reform agenda looks structural and contrasts with the voluntarist and initiatives-led policies which New Labour is currently pursuing in this Parliament.

Overcoming structural obstacles to reform

A fourth challenge is to reduce the deep and persistent inequalities in access to and outcomes from education and training: critical blocks to increased participation and achievement still exist. It is unlikely that supply-side interventions alone will be capable of generating the gear shift in performance required to match the levels of attainment achieved elsewhere in the world. Furthermore, incentives have to be created so that the population, as a whole, perceives that the struggle for education and training is worthwhile. In this respect, the English system has conspicuous historical weaknesses in the generally low employer demand for skills (Finegold and Soskise, 1988; Keep and Mayhew, 1997).

The Third Way as a reform agenda

What is ultimately at issue is how the Third Way translates into a reform agenda for post-compulsory education and training. Will it be based on individual responsibility, a voluntaristic and enabling state, relying on weak frameworks and keeping a close eye on the opinions of certain groups of voters? Or will the stress on individual responsibility be supported by a set of strong frameworks from a reforming state which seeks to mobilize and lead public opinion as well as tackling the more fundamental challenges of globalization? The early signs are that it is the former that is making the running, but as New Labour progresses through this Parliament, pressures may be building for the latter. Each of the following five chapters in this book examines what this might mean for constituent parts of the education and training system. Chapter 7 then considers what might be needed at a whole system level to make Third Way policies effective in the next Parliament.

Notes

1 We have chosen 14+, rather than the end of compulsory education at 16, as a point of demarcation for this book, on the grounds that the curriculum and qualifications at 14+ are increasingly seen as the starting point of a transition to adult and working life.
2 The following have been identified as features of the Fordist paradigm: mass production as a leading tendency in the economy; state intervention for macro-economic stabilization (Keynesianism); the idea of standardization and large-scale organizations; specialization; sharp divisions between mental and manual labour; emphasis on the producer rather than customer and so on (Murray, 1991).

2

Lifelong Learning and *The Learning Age*

Introduction

New Labour's second major education policy paper, *The Learning Age: A renaissance for a new Britain* (DfEE, 1998a), was published in February 1998 and lays out the Government's proposals for encouraging and supporting lifelong learning. This document, which was promised for the autumn and was billed as a White Paper, but finally emerged in the spring and was published as a Green Paper, received a cautious welcome for its scope and some of its proposals, but disappointed many because of its status as a Green Paper. Whatever the reasons for this change in status, the disappointment it caused is understandable, given – as Chapter 1 points out – the importance that New Labour has attached to lifelong learning as one of the central tenets of its economic and social policy.

The Green Paper illustrates many of the underlying themes of New Labour's approach to educational policy. First, it highlights the importance of lifelong learning as a key strategy for ensuring the future prosperity of the UK, but it envisages an enabling rather than a regulatory role for the state in supporting its development. Second, it underlines the importance of a partnership approach to lifelong learning, with a stress on the responsibilities of, as well as the opportunities for individuals, employers and trade unions to make the vision of a learning age a reality. Third, even though the New Deal[1] is not discussed in the Green Paper in any detail, there are allusions, in several places, to the important role of education and training in getting people off welfare and into work. Fourth, there is an emphasis on standards and quality. Finally, the policy proposals in *The Learning Age* reflect the constraints on public expenditure imposed by the Treasury in the first two years of government. They rely substantially on limited redistribution of existing resources, small amounts of new public funding for key initiatives and an increase in the amount of private funding being invested in education and training. What emerges is a document which has an inclusive and comprehensive vision of lifelong learning and emphasizes the importance of strategic planning, but consists of a series of individual initiatives in different sectors which together are intended to form a coherent whole.

What we will suggest in this chapter is that, although there are strong arguments for lifelong learning playing a key role in creating a more prosperous and equitable society in this country, there is a danger in assuming that education supply-side measures on their own are able to make lifelong learning a reality. While pursuing policies which make participation in learning appear more attractive to individual learners has undoubted benefits, unless these proposals are also supported by measures which relate directly to the labour market, they are unlikely to succeed in the long run. Although *The Learning Age* makes a clear connection between economic and education policies and highlights the importance of involving employers in its approach to lifelong learning, its policy proposals currently rely largely on educational solutions and a voluntarist approach to employers and to the labour market, rather than on legislation or a strong industrial policy. It remains to be seen whether this approach will deliver the policy outcomes New Labour requires to make the learning age it desires a reality.

Lifelong learning and *The Learning Age*: a new approach to education and training

Lifelong learning has become one of the key phrases in recent national policy documents on post-compulsory education and training, whether these originate from the previous administration or from New Labour. The term lifelong learning, which emphasizes the centrality of the learner rather than the provider and an on-going commitment to part-time learning rather than a short-term commitment to full-time initial education and training, can be seen as more than simply a new addition to the ever expanding list of educational jargon. Lifelong learning, as Chapter 1 argues, not only represents an 'organizing theme' of New Labour's education and training agenda, but is also seen as a major policy response to wider national and international economic and social changes.

Both the previous Conservative Government and the current Labour administration have stressed the necessity of developing lifelong learning and have drawn on international comparisons to demonstrate how economically successful nations appear to have benefited from a more concerted and co-ordinated approach to investment in human capital (DfE, 1995; DfEE, 1996; Labour Party, 1996a). In this country, developing lifelong learning, although originally largely seen as a way of addressing changing patterns of work organization and leisure, technological advances, globalization and skills deficits highlighted by international comparative studies, is increasingly now being used by New Labour as a strategic response to issues of equity and social cohesion (Kennedy, 1997; NCIHE, 1997; Fryer, 1997; DfEE, 1998a).

In the English context, the concept of a learning age, where learning throughout life becomes the norm rather than the exception, is therefore not only seen as one of the major ways of achieving economic success, but is also now being perceived as a mechanism with the potential to change national culture in relation to education and training (DfEE, 1998a). The idea that it is normal, or even possible in the current national and international context, to opt out of any kind of further education or training at the end of a period of compulsory education is increasingly being challenged. Recent national policy documents, such as the Kennedy Report (1997), Sir Ron Dearing's two reports on post-compulsory education and training (Dearing, 1996; NCIHE, 1997) and the two most recent reports on lifelong learning published under New Labour (Fryer, 1997; DfEE, 1998a), all stress the importance of individual commitment, as well individual entitlement to lifelong learning. There is a recognition that building a learning age in Britain will not be achieved without a new approach to education and training by government, by employers and by individual employees and learners.

Labour's major policy documents on education and training, both those written in opposition (Labour Party, 1996a; Labour Party, 1996c) and those published since coming to power in May 1997 (DfEE, 1997b; DfEE, 1998a), have all focused on the central importance of building a learning society and have attempted to translate this aspiration into practical proposals for encouraging lifelong learning. At the heart of these proposals lies the concept of a three-way partnership approach to lifelong learning by national government, employers and individuals. This partnership approach, which is designed to stimulate greater involvement in learning in as wide a variety of contexts as possible, recognizes the limitations of state intervention in this area and the importance of incentivizing learning for each of the key partners involved. This approach is by no means unique to the UK: according to the OECD Report on lifelong learning (OECD, 1996), it is very much in tune with what is happening in a large number of its member countries.

The partnership approach in the post-compulsory phase is built around the idea of shared responsibilities and shared benefits. There is a commitment by national government to focus on key enabling initiatives in this area, such as the University for Industry (UfI), New Deal and Individual Learning Accounts (ILAs), and to provide incentives for people of all ages and from all backgrounds to actively engage in education and training and thus in the creation of a more equitable and prosperous society. This is balanced by an expectation that individuals of all ages and at a number of different points in their lives will, of their own accord, take the opportunity to participate in different forms of learning in order to increase their economic and social well-being. Additionally, employers are exhorted to use their facilities and resources to provide access to and support for all types of learning and continuing professional development – not just job-specific training – as their contribution to a healthy economy and a better educated workforce for the future.

In many ways this approach differs very little from that put forward by the previous administration in *Lifetime Learning: A consultation document* (DfEE, 1995) and *Lifetime Learning: A policy framework* (DfEE, 1996). Indeed, several of New Labour's policy proposals in the area of lifelong learning, as we will point out later in this chapter, could be seen as a continuation of ideas that were put forward in these two documents. The difference between New Labour's policy documents in this area and those written when the Conservative Party was still in power, is, we would argue, subtle and contextual, but also important. By this we mean that the difference is largely one of tone and emphasis; it relies on stressing certain aspects of policy and downplaying others. For example, New Labour policy documents on education, training and lifelong learning stress equity and social cohesion rather than 'personal competitiveness' (DfEE, 1995). They emphasize the role that education and training play in citizenship formation as well as their role in skills formation and economic competitiveness. The documents also minimize the role of the market in stimulating demand for learning and highlight the importance of strategic regional and local planning and co-operation.

This approach might be seen as representing a move away from the domination of the market-led approach and the cult of individualism that characterized Conservative policies in this area, but also a departure from Old Labour's centralist regulatory approach to education and training and the labour market. There appears to be a recognition that supply-side measures and government-driven policies, on their own, are unlikely to succeed in the context of the late 1990s. It will be interesting to observe, over the lifetime of this Parliament, whether the subtle but important differences between New Labour's policies in this area and those of the previous administration eventually translate into a more successful approach to the building of a coherent lifelong learning strategy in this country.

Key challenges in the English context

Before looking at the specific policy proposals that the Labour Government is putting forward to support the concept of lifelong learning, it is important to look at some of the significant challenges that it faces in this area. These, we would suggest, are of two main types, both of which shape the context for reform. First, there are those challenges which result from education and training policy over the last 18 years and could be termed the Conservative legacy; secondly, there are wider economic, social and cultural factors which pose considerable deep-rooted obstacles to reform in the area of lifelong learning.

The Conservative legacy

If one looks at the current English education and training system as a whole in order to assess its viability as a structure for supporting lifelong learning, the outlook can appear somewhat bleak. It could be argued that the system's most notable feature is, in fact, its lack of coherence. As a result of minimal national, regional or local planning of post-compulsory education and training provision, together with market-driven and voluntarist approaches to education and training policy over the last 18 years, New Labour has inherited a system which does not immediately seem the ideal starting point for policies which are designed to promote lifelong learning (Robertson and Hillman, 1997a).

It is useful perhaps to consider the system from the learner's point of view: it is a salutary experience. Rather than being given access to a clearly defined and easily understood 'seamless robe' of provision or ladder of progressive learning opportunities, the potential lifelong learner is confronted by a range of competing autonomous institutions, often offering similar types of courses, but with a bewildering range of qualifications outcomes which do not automatically ensure access to a higher level of study. If the learner's objective is to gain some kind of specific work-related training, the picture may be more complex still, since responsibility for providing these kinds of learning opportunities is shared among an even greater range of providers, including employers, further education colleges, some higher education institutions, voluntary organizations, private training providers, trades unions and training and enterprise councils (TECs).

For younger learners there is an infrastructure of careers advisers and specialist careers teachers available to provide advice and guidance on the most appropriate education and training options, although in the competitive post-compulsory education market, there is some question over the impartiality of this advice (Schagen *et al*, 1996). For the adult learner, however, there is no such infrastructure. The quality or even existence of impartial advice and guidance varies significantly from locality to locality (Reisenberger and Sanders, 1997). There is often no one to help learners to find their way through the maze of programmes and qualifications on offer.

Once learners have identified what they might want to study, there may be considerable financial barriers to overcome in terms of funding that learning, unless they are young, able to study full-time and have the right credentials to qualify for a mandatory award. For adults, too, the costs of childcare, transport or materials for learning might well act as deterrents to participation in lifelong learning (Sargant *et al*, 1997).

The picture that one gets of the education and training system from the point of view of the learner, therefore, and particularly the adult part-time learner, is one not of coherence and opportunity, but rather one which exudes confusion and appears to throw up significant barriers to learning. It is hardly surprising, therefore, that three out of five adults claim that they have not participated in learning in the last three years (Sargant *et al*, 1997), that full-time and part-time participation in education and training at 16+ is low in this country, in comparison with the majority of other OECD countries (OECD, 1996), and that only 12 per cent of those in socio-economic groups IV and V gain a higher education qualification (NCIHE, 1997). As Tuckett (1997) says in his Foreword to *The Learning Divide*: 'Whilst the UK may aspire to transform itself into a learning society in which all participate, the experience on the ground is that the learning divide is as marked today as it has ever been. Age, class, previous educational experience and where you live all affect access to learning and the confidence to join in.'

The picture from the provider's side is also far from rosy. Although further education colleges and higher education institutions have seen an increasing proportion of adult learners over the last decade, until they now form a majority of the student body (Kennedy, 1997; NCIHE, 1997), a great deal of adult learning, particularly part-time learning, takes place in neither of these settings. Much of it goes on in the workplace, in the community, as part of LEA-funded adult education provision and in the home. Precisely because of the dispersed and disparate nature of this type of provision, it is difficult to track what is taking place in terms of volume, length or quality of study. There are success stories, such as the Open University, which continues to grow and flourish (NCIHE, 1997), and Employee Development Programmes, such as those at Ford or Unipart (Uden, 1996; Beattie, 1997), but there is also some evidence which provides less cause for optimism.

If one looks at employer-provided training, for example, the low uptake of Investors in People programmes by small and medium enterprises and the fact that the total number of training days provided by employers appears to have fallen sharply (Steedman and Green, 1996), the picture suggests that this is not currently an area of growth. If one adds to this concerns about the uneven availability of LEA-funded non-Schedule 2 adult education provision (Sargant, 1996), which is often used as a starting point back into education for many adults, cuts in LEA grants to voluntary organizations, the continuing uncertain quality of government-funded programmes for unemployed adults and the high number of adults who lack the basic skills required to access learning (Office of National Statistics, 1997), the probability of this country meeting even the limited adult-specific National Learning Targets[2] appears unlikely.

Wider factors

It would be quite unfair and also inaccurate, however, to attribute this gloomy picture solely to the previous administration's policies in education and training. There are a number of other wider and deep-seated economic, social and cultural problems which contribute to this country's failure to develop a culture of lifelong learning. These have been touched on in Chapter 1 and are well discussed and analysed in a number of key recent publications (eg Finegold and Soskise, 1988; Finegold, 1993; Keep and Mayhew, 1996a; Coffield, 1997). We do not, therefore, propose to go into them in any great detail here. However, it is perhaps important to highlight one or two of these wider economic, social and cultural factors to help to explain why, in Britain, we are so far from the concept of the 'learning age' to which New Labour clearly aspires in its recent Green Paper of that title (DfEE, 1998a).

Firstly, although the concept of lifelong learning has been discussed for some time in adult education circles (Tight, 1996), it has only become part of general policy discussion on education and training at a national level since the early 1990s. As the OECD Report *Lifelong Learning for All* (OECD, 1996: 27) points out: 'Although this notion of lifelong learning is now widely accepted, and has already become a natural feature of everyday life for certain privileged groups, the next essential step is to make it a reality for all.'

The idea that everyone not only has the opportunity to participate in learning throughout life, but that they also have the responsibility to do so in order to address some of the national and international challenges posed by global economic restructuring, demographic and lifestyle changes, is a relatively new concept for Britain. Here the focus on education and training has been front-loaded and exclusive. Until relatively recently, there has been an acceptance of low participation rates in post-compulsory education and training and the existence of highly selective qualifications designed to limit access to higher education (Finegold *et al*, 1990; Commission on Social Justice, 1994). Moreover, although employers have for some time expressed concern about the basic skills levels and work-readiness of potential recruits, as Unwin (1997) points out, unlike other countries, such as Germany, in Britain there is no real commitment to co-operation between education providers, government, employers and trade unions to provide a long-term or co-ordinated approach to work-based learning. Indeed, as Keep and Mayhew (1996b: 307) state in a recent analysis of British training policy over the last few years, many employers remain unconvinced of a direct link between training and profits 'which has important consequences for the success of an employer-led training strategy and for reliance on a market-based approach to investment in human capital'.

Selling the importance of investment in lifelong learning both to individuals, particularly to those who for social, economic, gender or racial reasons have traditionally been excluded, and to employers, including those in small and medium enterprises who have no tradition of training, clearly involves a considerable cultural shift in this country. New Labour will therefore need to get the balance between supply and demand for education, between individual choice and national policy objectives right if it is to create a sustainable system of lifelong learning. We would argue that to do this the Government will need to take a more integrated approach to education and labour market policies and to consider their interrelationship in a way that has not been fully explored or exploited by previous administrations. We would further suggest that there is a need for a strategic approach to creating a lifelong learning system, rather than relying on a series of laudable but potentially uncoordinated policy initiatives to stimulate lifelong learning. Given the English context, this might well require a more regulatory and less voluntarist approach to the labour market (see Chapters 4 and 7 for a more detailed discussion of the type of strong framework for new social partnership arrangements which this might require).

What an analysis of the past 18 years of Conservative education and training policy suggests is that relying on the market, voluntarism, supply-side measures, the concept of meritocracy and the idea of the 'trickle down effect' has neither created a culture of lifelong learning nor has it built a system to underpin it. In the English context, the need for a strong central policy drive to create a more coherent and transparent lifelong learning system, which is not only accessible to all, but is also attractive to all, must therefore be seen as an important objective for New Labour. In this context, a lifelong learning system which is 'attractive' means not only one which is appealing to learners of all ages, but one which is also valued, used, demanded and rewarded by employers. It is against these four criteria of coherence, transparency, accessibility and attractiveness that we propose to assess New Labour's education and training policy proposals for lifelong learning.

New Labour's proposals for building *The Learning Age*

As has been mentioned above, many of the policies that New Labour put forward in the area of lifelong learning while it was still in Opposition (Labour Party, 1996a) very much mirrored those outlined in the two contemporaneous DfEE policy documents on lifetime learning published under the Conservative administration (DfEE, 1995; DfEE, 1996). For example, there is support in New Labour documents for the National Targets for Education and Training (albeit in a revised form), for the Investors in People Initiative (although again in a revamped form), for Training and Enterprise Councils, for NVQs, for Vocational Training Tax Relief, for Modern Apprenticeships, for Employee Development Programmes, for a movement towards greater equity and consistency of funding for 16–19+ education provision, for more common quality assurance systems for providers of 16–19 education and training and for a focus on improving basic skills.

However, New Labour's pre-election policy documents and *The Learning Age* (DfEE, 1998a) also include proposals for changes in four areas – funding lifelong learning, the organization and planning of lifelong learning, work-based learning and qualifications reform – which differ quite significantly from those proposed by the Conservative administration. There is, too, a greater stress on the value of information and communications technologies (ICT) as a means of reaching out to people in their homes and workplaces as well as in traditional learning environments, which runs throughout the Green Paper. These proposals could all be seen as reflecting New Labour's specific concern with access and equity. They also appear to indicate a move away from market-led policies to a greater degree of strategic planning at the central and regional level. We will argue, however, that the Government policy proposals for creating a learning age cannot yet be considered as a coherent system for supporting lifelong learning, because they rely too heavily on a voluntarist rather than a more regulatory approach in this area.

Proposals for funding lifelong learning

In its most recent policy document, *The Learning Age* (DfEE, 1998a), New Labour puts forward a number of proposals for funding lifelong learning provision and for supporting learners to participate in lifelong learning which can be seen as directly designed both to increase and to widen access to learning.

There is a strong focus on targeting funding at those with the lowest qualifications levels (particularly those who need to improve their basic skills) and on the lowest incomes, while, at the same time, increasing the financial contributions of those who are likely to benefit most from the education system and have the ability to pay towards their education, such as university students from higher income families. This might be considered as part of New Labour's cautious redistribution agenda.

The major focus on funding in *The Learning Age*, however, is the proposal for the introduction of ILAs, which can be seen as supporting the concept of the partnership approach to lifelong learning referred to earlier in this chapter. 'Learning accounts will be built on two key principles; first, that individuals are best placed to choose what and how they want to learn; and second, that responsibility for investing in learning is shared' (DfEE, 1998a: 27).

ILAs, which were highlighted in New Labour policy documents prior to the election, and are given pride of place in *The Learning Age*, are seen as a mechanism for encouraging individuals to invest in their own education and training with support from the government and, in some cases, from their employers. There is an indication too that they could be used 'to make providers more responsive to learners' needs' (DfEE, 1998a: 26).

The details of how ILAs will be organized, what form they will take and whether eventually they will be provided on a universal or on a targeted basis is not spelt out in *The Learning Age*. There is, however, a clear commitment to their future development as a means of encouraging people to participate in learning. The Green Paper also announces a £150 million pilot project to test out how ILAs might work in practice.

ILAs were first mooted in the Commission on Social Justice Report

(1994) and based on many of the ideas which had been developed earlier by Miliband (1991) and Robertson (1994). The Report proposed that all learners should have access to ILAs and that all employers would be required either to invest a minimum proportion of each employee's earnings in training (eg 1 to 1.5 per cent in the first instance) or to pay into a common fund for training at TEC level or through their employees' ILAs. ILAs would be administered through a Learning Bank, which would manage the mix of government, individual learner and employer funds required to resource all types of post-compulsory provision. There would be no distinction between levels or types of learning, so learners could both invest in and draw on their ILAs as and when their learning needs emerged. The Learning Bank and the Individual Learning Account, it was claimed, would help to reduce the inequity of current national government funding regimes which favour younger full-time learners taking academic courses over older part-time learners on unaccredited or vocational courses. In such a system, all types of learning would be broken down into units or modules with credit attached, which learners could accumulate through a variety of modes of study over a period of time in order to gain a nationally recognized qualification. This credit-based system would form the basis for the funding structure of the Learning Bank and funding would follow the learner rather than be given as a block grant to education or training providers.

The concept of the ILA as laid out in both pre-election Labour documents (Labour Party, 1996a, 1996d) and in *The Learning Age* (DfEE, 1998a) differs from that set out in the Commission on Social Justice Report in four significant ways. First, it appears likely that ILAs will not initially be on offer to all learners, but will be targeted at certain groups of people, who will receive £150 from the government towards the cost of their learning. Second, there is no compulsion on employers to contribute to their employees' ILAs – Labour appears very wary of introducing the type of levy system described in the Commission on Social Justice Report. Third, there is no firm commitment by the Labour Party to the idea of a Learning Bank which would administer the ILA and the funding of all post-compulsory provision. Finally, there is no clear link between the concept of ILAs and a system of credit accumulation and transfer.

What the Labour Party does commit itself to in both its pre-election policy documents and in its first Green Paper in this area is far less radical and comprehensive. It is merely a commitment to a practical consideration of how ILAs might be used as a tool to distribute post-compulsory learning opportunities more equitably, to incentivize learning for individuals and to increase employers' active involvement in educating and training their workforces.

A detailed proposal for ILAs and the Learning Bank was initially outlined by Robertson (1995) and then developed in some depth by Robertson and Hillman in the Report of the National Committee of Inquiry into Higher Education (Robertson and Hillman, 1997a), as well as in a number of recent journal articles by Robertson (1996a, 1996b, 1997c). In all of these, there is support for the concept, particularly as a way of giving learners more 'purchasing power' in the education and training market and as a more equitable means of funding higher education provision. ILAs are seen as one mechanism for ensuring the expansion of and encouraging the widening of participation in higher education, as well as a way of providing the increased funding that the sector urgently needs in order to avoid rationalization of higher education places.

The use of ILAs to fund all types of provision, including vocational education and training, however, receives less support from Robertson, who has concerns about how far such a mechanism would influence the structure of the learning market at this level (Robertson, 1996a). In particular, he is concerned that a system of ILAs should be protected in its start-up phase from the kind of failure that the Training Credits scheme experienced: namely, the unemployed, who were invited to take up the credits for training but were never in a position to influence its supply. He suggests, therefore, that any Learning Bank pilots should take place first in the higher education sector and should perhaps begin by absorbing the Student Loans Company (Robertson, 1996b). This suggestion has not been taken up in either *The Learning Age* or its accompanying document *Higher Education for the 21st Century: Response to the Dearing Report* (DfEE, 1998b).

Alongside the proposal for the piloting of ILAs, which is clearly seen as one of the most important potential mechanisms for funding lifelong learning, *The Learning Age* also includes a number of proposals for supporting individuals to participate in learning. These are designed not only to support those on low incomes, but also to make it more attractive for those on benefits to undertake education and training to improve their employability skills. Proposals include an increase in the size of the access fund for students in further and higher education, an amendment to the Jobseeker's Allowance, so that those who are unemployed can study for up to a year full-time and only need to be available for work outside term time; and changes in the benefit rules for those on Workskill pilot projects.

The most controversial of New Labour's funding proposals for lifelong learning are still, undoubtedly, those which relate to tuition fees for younger adults in higher education. These proposals, which have received considerable criticism in the press and have led to heated debate in both Houses of Parliament and to demonstrations by students and lecturers in higher education, will be discussed in more detail in Chapter 5.

Taken together, New Labour's proposals for funding lifelong learning can be seen as a positive attempt to create incentives for a wider group of learners to participate in learning and to try to ensure that the welfare system supports it, rather than creating barriers for those on benefit to undertake education and training. In this sense, the funding proposals in *The Learning Age* can be seen as part of the Government's redistribution agenda, but it is a redistribution agenda which is designed to stress individual responsibility and commitment to lifelong learning, rather than a move in the direction of coercion or statutory duty to provide education and training. As David Blunkett, Secretary of State for Education and Employment, states in his Foreword to *The Learning Age,* 'The Learning Age will be built on a renewed commitment to self-improvement and on a recognition of the enormous contribution learning makes to our lives' (DfEE, 1998a: 8).

It remains to be seen whether this individual commitment to and recognition of the value of lifelong learning will be enough to stimulate the kind of demand for learning that Blunkett so evidently both believes exists and which the type of funding policies set out in *The Learning Age* require to make lifelong learning a reality.

Proposals for the planning and organization of lifelong learning

One area where both the education and training policy documents New Labour published prior to its election in May 1997 and the two that it has published since that date – *Excellence in Schools* (DfEE, 1997b) and *The Learning Age* (DfEE, 1998a) – differ strongly from those published by the Conservative administration is in the area of the planning and organization of lifelong learning. Planning was a word which the Conservative Government, with its faith in the power of the market and individual choice and its horror of LEAs, avoided in all its documents about education and training.

Both *Learn as You Earn: Labour's plans for a skills revolution* (Labour Party, 1996d) and *Lifelong Learning* (Labour Party, 1996a), however, spell out the dangers of an approach to education and training which relies on the market rather than on strategic planning by central and local government to ensure adequate and high quality education and training provision. These documents then go on to suggest the need for more strategic planning at the regional and local levels in order to provide some sort of coherent framework of provision for lifelong learning and to counteract some of the problems that have arisen from competition between post-16 providers.

The Learning Age, while putting forward proposals for a more collaborative and strategic approach to planning in its chapter entitled 'Realizing the Learning Age', does not contain the same kind of critique of voluntarism as is contained in New Labour's pre-election policy documents. In this chapter there is encouragement for local partners (LEAs, post-16 providers and TECs) to work with the FEFC and the Local Government Association to develop 'more coherent planning and funding arrangements in post-16 education' (DfEE, 1998a: 47) supported by a Collaboration Fund for post-16 providers. More radically, there is an indication that competition should give way to more coherent local provision and shared facilities: 'The development of a collaborative network of tertiary education is a long-term objective of the Government.'

Local partnership, particularly around the setting up of local learning centres, is also seen as crucial to the impact and effectiveness of two of Labour's key ICT-based lifelong learning policy proposals – the University for Industry and the National Grid for Learning.

Alongside its proposals for local planning and collaboration, *The Learning Age* begins to spell out New Labour's plans for strategic regional planning which will be co-ordinated through Regional Development Agencies (RDAs). Although the role for the RDAs is only briefly outlined in the Green Paper, it is clear that these new bodies are seen as having a central part to play in co-ordinating and planning an interrelated economic and education policy at the regional level. It is proposed that the RDAs will be responsible for such tasks as tackling skills shortage, identifying future skill needs, supporting local partnerships through the Single Regeneration Budget Challenge Fund, ensuring that regional economic and labour market trends influence decisions about training and careers education and guidance and encouraging inward investment for supporting learning.

The trailing of RDAs in *The Learning Age* has been followed swiftly by the publication of a White Paper *Building Partnerships for Prosperity* (DETR, 1997) and legislation to establish RDA Boards in all regions in 1998 so that RDAs can become fully operational in April 1999, with the exception of London where the aim is to establish the RDA in April 2000 at the same time as the new strategic authority.

A further recent development in this area is the Secretary of State's announcement of plans for Strategic Lifelong Learning Partnerships supported by a new Partnership Fund worth £25 million over the three years from 1999–2002 (DfEE, 1999a). Lifelong learning partnerships, which were initially proposed in *Lifelong Learning* (Labour Party, 1996a) are seen as a mechanism for bringing greater coherence to local learning provision and to student support arrangements. These partnerships between schools, colleges, LEAs, Careers Service and TECs, will also be responsible for setting local learning targets related to the National Learning Targets for young people and adults (DfEE, 1999b).

As Chapter 7 points out, it is in the area of strategic planning at the regional and local levels that there appears to be both the clearest departure from Conservative policy in terms of lifelong learning and New Labour's greatest potential opportunity for bringing together economic and education policy to create the right kind of balance between supply and demand for lifelong learning.

There are two other areas related to the planning and organization of lifelong learning, however, where those who have campaigned specifically on behalf of adult learners are bound to be critical of *The Learning Age*. First, the Green Paper fails to address the issues raised by the long-standing debate about the importance of defining 'adequate provision' in terms of non-Schedule 2 adult education. Second, apart from the Learning Direct Telephone Line to provide advice and guidance for learners of all ages, *The*

Learning Age is short on proposals for improving guidance on learning and work for adults, although this issue is more fully addressed in a more recent consultation paper, *Local Information, Advice and Guidance for Adults in England – Towards a National Framework* (DfEE, 1998c).

Proposals for work-based learning

As indicated earlier, one of the major challenges for creating a learning age in this country is increasing the quality and quantity of work-based learning and involving employers more actively in strategies for lifelong learning. It is undoubtedly for this reason that the chapter on the University for Industry (UfI) and the chapter entitled 'Learning at Work' are situated so centrally and are accorded such space in the Government's Green Paper on lifelong learning. In addition, the Government has published a separate prospectus on the UfI (DfEE, 1998d) and has strongly promoted and financially supported its New Deal for unemployed 18–24-year-olds initiative.

The New Deal initiative will form the subject of Chapter 3 in this book and will thus not be considered here. In this chapter, we will focus on the proposals for stimulating and supporting work-based learning for adults as outlined in *The Learning Age*. Foremost among these is the proposal for the establishment of the UfI.

The UfI was originally mooted in a speech by Gordon Brown in 1994 (Brown, 1994), began to make an appearance in Labour Party policy documents on lifelong learning in 1996 (Labour Party, 1996a, 1996d) and was then critically explored as a concept by the Institute for Public Policy Research (Hillman, 1996), before emerging as one of the key lifelong learning initiatives of New Labour in government (DfEE, 1998a, 1998d).

According to the Secretary of State for Education and Employment, David Blunkett, the UfI is seen as a mechanism which will 'offer access to a learning network to help people deepen their knowledge, update their skills and gain new ones' (DfEE, 1998a: 8).

It is essentially intended to act as a broker between learners and learning opportunities, whether these are delivered in a specific educational setting or via information and communications technologies directly into the home or the workplace. The UfI will, therefore, provide a front line service of advice and guidance about learning opportunities and learning providers to learners and employers through its telephone line, Learning Direct; co-ordinate the setting up of a network of learning centres in accessible locations around the country; publicize the importance of learning; identify gaps in provision; commission specific learning packages or provision to satisfy learners' demands; and quality assure the products and services to which it provides access.

In the *University for Industry Pathfinder Prospectus* (DfEE, 1998d) it is suggested that there will be a membership system for the UfI. Individual members will be registered and given a lifetime record which will store information about past qualifications, interests and requirements for learning and will be regularly updated as the learner achieves new qualifications or awards. Corporate members will receive a similar service, but in this case the emphasis will be on self-assessment of their organizations' learning needs.

Once the UfI Transition Team has been set up with Government start-up funding, the UfI is gradually expected to become both independent, with its own permanent Chief Executive, and self-financing through contributions from employers, learning providers and learners themselves. There is an indication, however, that public sector funding will continue to support the needs of particular learners. Initially, the UfI is expected to prioritize learning related to literacy, numeracy and ICT, the development of skills in small and medium enterprises, and skills needs in specific sectors (eg automotive components, environmental technology) and services, although the intention is that all learners, regardless of age, level of education or employment status, should be able to make use of the UfI as a way of accessing learning. The UfI will work with both national partners, such as employer federations and National Training Organizations (NTOs), and local partners, such as TECs and local education providers, to ensure a co-ordinated approach to learning at all levels.

One concern about the UfI is whether there is an infrastructure for delivering open learning of the type required by this initiative. A recent National Extension College and *Times Education Supplement* survey of further education colleges' readiness to offer open and distance learning (Nash and Nicholls, 1997), discovered that almost one third of further education, sixth-form and adult education colleges do not currently offer any kind of open or distance learning. Even those colleges that have developed this type of provision have usually done it on a very small scale. Only six institutions that responded to the survey had more than 1,000 students studying through open or distance learning; the majority had 500 or less and in 19 of the colleges, fewer than 50 students were able to use open or distance learning facilities.

However, there is some interesting evidence emerging from the recent UfI pilot project which has been run independently of Government by the IPPR and the University of Sunderland. A network of 35 learning centres was established in the Tyne and Wear area, linked to a central database accessible via a call-centre and Web site. Partners included local colleges, the BBC, the FEFC and the NHS Executive.

During the 13 months of the project, there was a total of 7,868 registrations, of which 6,123 were for 'tasters', with particular interest being shown in ICT. Nearly one quarter of the registrations were by Internet, direct from people at home, work or in a learning centre which was supported by staff. While this initial interest can be seen as a considerable success, the pilot was less successful in ensuring learner progression or engaging small and medium enterprises to take part. What the pilot project did demonstrate, however, was that commercial marketing techniques can reach learners across all social classes. It also developed a sophisticated infrastructure for the UfI as a 'learning broker' (Milner *et al*, 1999).

One further major challenge for the UfI is exactly how it will assure the quality of the provision that it offers, particularly when it begins to use a wide range of private training organizations or consultants, as well as state-funded and regularly inspected education and training providers. This is something which the pilot project was not able to explore in any depth.

The proposals for the UfI exemplify the Government's clearly supportive but voluntarist approach to all types of learning at work: 'Transforming learning in the workplace will primarily be for employers, employees and the self-employed to achieve. The Government will help people to invest in learning by lifting barriers to access and improving the quality of support available to businesses and individuals' (DfEE, 1998a: 33).

Although this statement goes on to talk about combining 'effective pressure and support within an effective legislative framework', there is very little evidence of this legislative framework within the 'Learning at Work' chapter of the Green Paper. The only two examples of such a framework which are cited in the document are the legislation which entitles all 16 and 17-year-old employees to undertake education and training up to NVQ Level 2 (if they are not already there); and the maintenance of the statutory powers of the Construction Industry Training Board and the Engineering Construction Industry Training Board to raise a levy from employers to fund training. The first example is permissive and therefore relies on employees asserting their rights rather than on employers being forced to release their young employees. The second could be seen as a very weak sop to those on the Left who supported old Labour's proposals for a training levy on employers.

Nevertheless, there are a number of important, and in some cases innovative, proposals for supporting work-based learning for adults in this chapter of the Green Paper. These include the establishment of a National Skills Task Force to assess future skill needs and tackle skill shortages, the designation of five Employment Zones to combat long-term unemployment, plans for the setting up of 37 NTOs to promote lifelong learning in different sectors (including a Management and Enterprise NTO to encourage the development of management skills and courses) and the introduction of a number of Workskill pilot projects designed to test out how changes in benefit rules on education and training can assist the unemployed to get and retain a job. These initiatives are discussed in more detail in Chapter 4.

Arguably one of the most significant sections in this chapter of the Green Paper, and one which contains proposals that mark a clean break from policies associated with the previous administration, is the one on trade unions. New Labour clearly sees a role for trade unions as social partners in the drive to promote lifelong learning in the workplace. To encourage trade unions to carry out this role, the Government will provide a total of £8 million during the period 1998–2001 to support Employee Education Development Schemes. In addition, there is support for the TUC's Bargaining for

Skills initiative, which helps trade union representatives to negotiate with employers about improved training opportunities for their members.

Proposals for qualifications reform

The fourth area which New Labour addresses in its Green Paper on lifelong learning and which was not addressed in the Conservative policy papers on lifetime learning, is the area of qualifications reform. Chapter 6 of *The Learning Age* briefly tackles the role of qualifications in recognizing achievement and encouraging lifelong learning and puts forward a number of policy proposals for reforming qualifications in order to ensure that they are equal to fulfilling this role. It is recognized, for example, that there is a need for qualifications to record 'smaller steps of achievement' (DfEE, 1998a: 63) and that adults (but not young people?) may need to 'build up recognition for bits of learning at a time'(DfEE, 1998a: 66). This leads up to a cautious proposal for developing a unitized credit framework within further education, although it is unclear what is meant here by further education and whether it includes learners of all ages. It is also unfortunately transparently clear that this credit framework does not embrace higher education programmes and does not therefore cover all learners in one coherent system.

Although the policy proposals on qualifications reform in *The Learning Age* are brief, somewhat tentative and appear to consider qualifications for adults and for young people as two separate entities, the fact that a national qualifications system is seen as part of the essential infrastructure for lifelong learning is undoubtedly a useful step in the direction of a system approach to lifelong learning (see Chapter 6 for a more detailed discussion of this issue).

How New Labour's policy proposals match up to the challenge of creating a learning age

Earlier in this chapter, we attempted to describe both what lies behind New Labour's concept of a learning age and also the importance of the strategy of lifelong learning to this concept. We also suggested that the current education and training system in England and Wales displays a number of characteristics which tend to discourage rather than to encourage lifelong learning and which could thus be seen as barriers to the development of a learning age. This, we argued, was the result of the Conservative education policy legacy and of wider economic, social and cultural factors, both of which pose a considerable challenge for New Labour. We suggested that any policy proposals which the new administration put forward for reform of the education and training system would need to address issues of coherence, transparency, accessibility and attractiveness to learners if they were to succeed in supporting and stimulating lifelong learning. It is against these criteria, therefore, that we propose to assess New Labour's policies in the area of lifelong learning.

The challenge of coherence

Previous sections of this chapter have indicated just how fragmented and incoherent the education and training system is at present, whether it is viewed from a learner's, a provider's or a whole-system perspective. There are a number of hopeful signs in *The Learning Age* (DfEE, 1998a), however, that this is an issue which the new administration not only recognizes that it needs to address, but where it also has some concrete policy proposals to offer.

This document, like Labour's pre-election policy papers before it, indicates a commitment to a more strategic planned approach to developing a lifelong learning system. It emphasizes the importance of regional planning and the links between education and the labour market; the strategic role of local partnerships; and the need for inter-agency working to tackle issues of access to and support for lifelong learning. The Adult and Community Learning Fund and the Collaboration Fund, for example, are both seen as incentives (albeit small) for different and previously competing providers to co-operate over local provision to meet the Government's long-term objective of 'a collaborative network of tertiary education' (DfEE, 1998a: 47). At the national level, the National Skills Task Force has been set up to support this type of local and regional planning and to monitor and tackle current and future skills needs.

This is certainly a far cry from the type of policies pursued by the previous administration in an attempt to create a market in education and training. However, there is also still a long way to go before further, higher and adult education and training providers are all seen as equally important and equally valued parts of a coherent and unified post-compulsory education and training system offering potential learners access to a seamless robe of lifelong learning opportunities. Moreover, the degree of competitiveness between the different sectors and the different providers within each sector is still acute (Russell, 1997e). The proposed RDAs will have to be armed with some strong financial incentives, as well as convincing plans and targets for their given areas, if coherence and collaboration are going to win out over fragmentation and competition. Recent guidance on RDAs provides advice on how these organizations might work (DETR, 1998) but there is no discussion of funding or resources.

Perhaps more worryingly, the policy proposals which are put forward in Chapter 3 of *The Learning Age* – 'Learning at Work' – still look very much like a collection of interesting and potentially useful initiatives, rather than a coherent strategy for work-based learning. There is a great deal of reliance on ICT solutions in this area and on the efficacy of the UfI and ILAs. The proposals also rest heavily on gaining employer, trade union and employee support, rather than on providing a statutory framework and strong infrastructure of frameworks for work-based education and training. As indicated earlier in this chapter, we feel that there are dangers in this voluntarist approach. Only time will tell whether reservations about New Labour's approach in this area are well founded. We return to this important issue in both Chapters 4 and 7.

The challenge of transparency

Earlier in this chapter we pointed out how difficult it is for learners to make sense of the current post-compulsory education and training system, not only because of its internal incoherence, but also because of its lack of transparency. There is a sense in which the search for transparency may well become the search for the holy grail, if you are talking about the complexity of a system such as that required to support lifelong learning. What may be required in such a system are structures or frameworks which provide a pathway through the complexity.

Many education policy commentators have seen a unitized and comprehensive national credit framework as one mechanism which would help to make the system for lifelong learning more transparent to learners (eg Wilson, 1993; Robertson, 1994; Stanton, 1997). Such a framework, it is argued, would allow all learning to be described and measured in a common form, regardless of the context in which it was being achieved. It would thus help learners to make sense of their learning in relation to all other types of learning and to have learning achieved and accredited in one learning environment recognized in another.

Pre-election Labour education policy documents (eg Labour Party, 1996a, 1996b) appear to attach considerable importance to developing a national credit framework. As we have indicated above, however, *The Learning Age* is much more tentative on this point and clearly sees a separate credit system for further education. This concept of a separate credit system for different parts of the system is reinforced, in terms of 16–19-year-olds, by the Government's response to the *Qualifying for Success* consultation process (DfEE, 1998e); and, for higher education, by the DfEE's response to the National Commission of Inquiry into Higher Education Report (DfEE, 1998b). It does not appear, therefore, that New Labour is now putting forward proposals for a single national credit framework; rather what seems to be emerging are two separate systems in further and higher education, both of which exclude 16–19-year-olds. It is difficult to see how these policy proposals support the concept of lifelong learning or make the education and training system more transparent to learners.

The challenge of accessibility

The arguments for the need to make the education and training system in this country more accessible for different types of learners at different points in their life is, of course, far from a new one; it is just that it has been brought into sharper focus with the current emphasis on lifelong learning.

If it is to encourage lifelong learning, the education and training system in this country self-evidently needs to be one which is accessible to all ages, although the mechanisms that are used to support accessibility may well be different for different ages and at different stages in a learner's life. Policies for combating early disaffection and non-participation, we would argue, should be seen as part of the same strategy as policies designed to make the education and training system more accessible for adult learners.

What current studies of adult participation (eg Sargant *et al*, 1997; RSA, 1996) demonstrate is that the single most important indicator of whether individuals will continue to access education and training throughout their lives is their level of achievement in initial education and training. To see this stage of education as separate from continuing education and training is unhelpful therefore – the two are clearly deeply interrelated and interdependent.

Having said that the challenge of accessibility is one which relates as much to initial as to continuing education and training, the focus in this section of the chapter will largely relate to the latter, since initial education and training is discussed in more depth in other chapters of this book.

If one looks at New Labour's recent policy documents in the area of lifelong learning, there are a number of indications that this administration takes the issue of accessibility for adults very seriously. The two 'big ideas' – the University for Industry and the Individual Learning Account – can both be seen as promoting accessibility: the first through the use of new technologies designed to reach out to people in their communities, as well as in the workplace; and the second through the use of financial incentives to participate. In addition, there are proposals to support family and community learning schemes and adults wishing to improve their basic skills, including their computer literacy skills (DfEE, 1997; DfEE, 1998a). In terms of higher education, there are a number of concrete proposals which demonstrate New Labour's emphasis on making the education and training system more accessible. The cap on the number of students entering higher education, for example, which was imposed by the previous administration, has been lifted. Also, the HEFCE has been advised to give priority to those institutions 'which can demonstrate a commitment to widening access' (DfEE, 1998b: 12) and to fund projects for widening access and participation.

These proposals, taken together with a number of New Labour's other proposals for supporting learners within the education and training system, can be seen as evidence of New Labour's commitment to improving access to lifelong learning opportunities. However, there is still a concern about the Government's failure to fulfil its pre-election promise to define the concept of 'adequacy' in relation to non-Schedule 2 adult provision, and thus its failure to ensure greater equality of access to informal or unaccredited provision which is, for many adults, the first step back to more formal education and training (Sargant, 1996; Reisenberger and Sanders, 1997). A further major issue, already mentioned above, is the lack of concrete proposals for ensuring that adults have access to high quality individual advice and guidance about lifelong learning opportunities – surely a key element of accessibility.

Since the publication of *The Learning Age*, however, there have been encouraging signs that the Government has recognized the central importance of advice and guidance to the success of its lifelong learning project. A recent consultation paper entitled *Local Information, Advice and Guidance for Adults in England – Towards a National Framework* (DfEE, 1998c), which proposes a framework of both free initial information and advice followed up by a purchasable service of more in-depth guidance, is a welcome addition to the original Green Paper. The proposals in this document signal a desire to build on the best of existing local practice and, as in many other areas of policy, to use local partnerships to deliver a service to potential adult learners.

The challenge of attractiveness

In much of what has been written above about coherence, transparency and accessibility, there has been a focus on education and training policy and the type of changes that can be made to the education and training system to support these concepts. Once one begins to look at the issue of attractiveness, however, wider economic, social and cultural factors which can, to a certain extent, be ignored or pushed into second place in discussions about coherence, transparency and accessibility, suddenly become central to the debate. It could be argued that making the education and training system attractive enough to encourage lifelong learning is perhaps the hardest objective to achieve, particularly since, as we have argued earlier in this chapter, there are strong economic, social and cultural reasons why learners in this country have not traditionally participated to such a great extent as learners in many other countries (OECD, 1996; Steedman and Green, 1997). Moreover, as we pointed out above, it is not only learners for whom the concept of lifelong learning has to be attractive; it also needs to be recognized, valued and supported by public and private employers, who have a key part to play in the practical realization of the concept.

What then is the New Labour administration proposing to do which will attract learners and employers to participate in the joint project of developing lifelong learning? The Government's policy documents suggest two major ways in which this problem might be tackled, both of which reflect our earlier analysis of its approach in this area – exhortation combined with financial incentives.

First, they suggest raising the profile of the debate on lifelong learning and the learning age and there is some evidence of action on this front. A minister responsible for lifelong learning (currently Rt Hon George Mudie) has been appointed, an Advisory Committee on Lifelong Learning has been set up and has produced its first report (Fryer, 1997) and there has been a Green Paper devoted to lifelong learning. Second, there is an emphasis on using financial incentives to encourage individuals and employers to participate in lifelong learning.

However, there are those who argue that these types of policies which focus primarily on the education and training system, but do nothing to regulate the labour market, are doomed to failure (Keep and Mayhew, 1996a; Keep and Mayhew, 1996b; Coffield, 1997). Making the education system more coherent, transparent, accessible and attractive only goes so far in terms of stimulating demand for learning. Education and training policies need to be matched by labour market policies to ensure that those who participate in learning are rewarded in some way by the labour market for their efforts. Building a learning society requires more than supply-side policies. Piecemeal incentives to stimulate participation in lifelong learning and to make learning more accessible are unlikely on their own to bring about the real cultural change in attitudes to learning that the vision of a learning age demands. In order to bring about this kind of radical change, the Government will also have to consider how it can ensure that the labour market both rewards the fruits of learning and encourages those who have gained higher skills to participate more fully in building the high skills economy which the Government claims it wishes to create.

Key areas for further development

There are, we would argue, a number of key areas which require further development if this administration is to make lifelong learning more of a reality for more people. We have divided these areas into those which could and should be tackled in the short term and those which require longer-term measures. There is a bias towards policies which relate to education and training, because that is the specific focus of this book. However, as stated above, we recognize the vital importance of arguments for complementary labour market and welfare reform policies. Many of these measures might be seen as remedial or compensatory rather than visionary. This is because of the low baseline from which this country is starting in this area, but also because there is a need to build equity into a system which has traditionally been exclusive.

Short-term measures

First, there is a need to raise the profile of the debate about lifelong learning at national level through effective use of the media and through ensuring that relevant statistical information is collected to inform this debate. Equally importantly, there is a need to work at the other end of the scale with individuals, families and communities and through the provision of high quality, accessible and ongoing guidance and advice. The focus in both cases will be on the need both to participate in education and training and to be prepared to contribute more to its costs in the knowledge of the benefits that accrue from it. However, safeguards will need to be built into the system for those who are unable, for whatever reason, to contribute to the costs of their participation in lifelong learning and these will need to be widely advertised and understood.

Second, it is important to continue to focus on improving the basic skills of adults, as well as children, and these should include not only literacy and numeracy but also English as a Second Language and Information and Communications Technology. Improving the basic skills of the population needs to be seen as an important part of regional strategic plans for education and training. There should be specific local targets in this area, as well as strategies for meeting these targets, which include community projects, such as the very successful family literacy schemes and self-help groups, as well as more formal education and workplace initiatives. The Moser Committee work in this area is a welcome start and will be vital to the future development of a basic skills strategy.

Third, there should be a strong emphasis on regional planning of post-compulsory education and training which is designed to diminish the worst effects of institutional competition without removing the power of institutions to respond creatively to their local markets and the needs of the local economy (Pearce and Hillman, 1998).

Fourth, there is a need to highlight and build on initiatives, such as employee development programmes, the Open University, the University of the Third Age and Adult Learners' Week, which have successfully managed to widen participation in learning.

Fifth, it is important to get tax and other financial incentives for individuals and employers right to encourage participation in education and training while, at the same time, ensuring that the benefit system works in tandem with education and training policy to support investment in learning.

Sixth, if the education and training system is to begin to change in the way that it needs to in order to support lifelong learning, it will be necessary to prepare teachers, lecturers and trainers for that change. It is therefore important that staff development for those in post-compulsory education and training is seen not only as the key to enhanced quality of delivery in the sector as a whole, but also as an inherent feature of any kind of policy proposals designed to promote or support lifelong learning.

Finally, and linked to the previous point, there will need to be a real focus on the type of pedagogy which best supports lifelong learning (Hodgson and Kambouri, 1999). This is an area which is barely touched on in New Labour's policy documents, except possibly in relation to ICT. Yet it is clear that if more people, with more diverse needs and in a wider variety of settings are going to be participating in learning at different stages of their lives, then the type of pedagogy that is currently employed is unlikely to be equal to the task.

Longer-term issues

In the longer term, there will be more fundamental structural issues to face in terms of building the kind of seamless robe of provision required for a system of lifelong learning, as well as the kind of social and economic climate in which learning is valued, used and rewarded. We suggest that there are four areas which require attention: building a unified, progressive and inclusive 14+ curriculum and qualifications system; creating a strategy for the development of skills at Levels 3 and 4, as well as at Levels 1 and 2; ensuring that there is a better balance between work, education and family life; and developing stronger links between education, training and the world of work so that the labour market recognizes and rewards those who participate in education and training. We will return to a discussion of these issues in subsequent chapters.

The problem with developing policies to stimulate lifelong learning is that there is a need to work on a number of fronts at the same time. It is no good to stimulate demand for learning if there is a shortage of high quality provision to satisfy the varying individual needs that have been awoken; equally there is no use in improving the quality of provision, if there is no demand for it. Moreover, short-term incentives to participate in lifelong learning will be doomed to failure if individual commitment is not rewarded by real longer-term benefits, such as better employment opportunities, more involvement in decision-making, improved self esteem and enhanced social prospects. Building a learning age is a formidable task because it involves winning hearts and minds, as well as putting into place practical strategies in a number of related areas which together will turn rhetoric into reality. On the other hand, the potential gains to be derived from it are enormous and could establish the basis for a more equitable, peaceful, culturally vibrant and economically viable society for the 21st century.

Creating a learning age is something which will take considerably longer than one term of Parliament. Perhaps the New Labour administration should, therefore, be judged on whether the policies that it introduces in its first term of Government begin to put into place the frameworks required for a future system of lifelong learning. The jury is out.

Notes

1 Because of its central importance to New Labour's approach to social and educational reform, the New Deal forms the focus of a chapter on its own in this book and is thus not discussed in any detail here.

2 The National Learning Targets for the Year 2002 which relate specifically to adults are: 50 per cent of adults with a Level 3 qualification and 28 per cent with a Level 4 qualification; 45 per cent of large/medium-sized organizations and 10,000 small organizations recognized as IiP (NACETT, 1998).

3

The New Deal and the 'Lost Generation'

Introduction

This chapter examines New Labour's Welfare to Work strategy and its New Deal programmes. Because the prime concern of these policies is to tackle the problem of long-term unemployment with all its attendant issues of poverty and social exclusion, the chapter does not confine itself solely to matters of education and training, but necessarily crosses boundaries into discussion of the economy, employment and welfare reform. The chapter begins with a broad description of New Labour's approach in this area and the various New Deal programmes it has introduced. We then focus on the operation of the New Deal for 18–24-year-olds and, to a lesser extent, on the 25 Plus New Deal. In the final part of the chapter, we look at some of the significant current and future challenges for the successful operation of these programmes. We conclude that while the New Deal may be achieving some success in moving young people from benefit and into work, we note that there are significant operational issues still to be tackled. Moreover, New Labour will have to face wider 'system' and economic issues if it is to solve the problem of long-term unemployment.

Welfare to Work, New Deal and New Labour's political priorities

The Welfare to Work strategy is a central pillar of New Labour's overall political approach for this Parliament as it seeks to address the issue of the 'lost generation'. This refers to a group of young people who, under the Conservative Government, did not stay on at school or college or become part of quality work-based training programmes, but drifted into long-term unemployment and benefit dependency. The Welfare to Work strategy is, therefore, designed to address the issue of long-term unemployment, break the spiral of escalating spending on social security and end the dependency culture.

Within the Welfare to Work strategy are various New Deal programmes, the most high profile of which is the New Deal for 18–24-year-olds. In addition, there are New Deal programmes for those over 25, for lone parents and for those with disabilities. In this chapter, we will deal primarily with the New Deal for 18–24-year-olds and for those over 25, because of their relationship to the overall education and training strategy of New Labour.

The concept of the New Deal is full of political symbolism for the Social Democratic Left. It is the same term as that used to describe the policies of the Democrat president, Franklin D Roosevelt, in tackling mass unemployment in the United States in the 1930s. Sixty years later, David Blunkett, Secretary of State for Education, talked emotively of a 'national crusade to give the young and long-term unemployed an opportunity to learn, to earn and to acquire new skills' (Blunkett, 1997).

However, New Labour's concept of the New Deal is different from the concept behind Franklin D Roosevelt's programme. The New Deal of the US in the 1930s was a non-militarist reflation of the economy, in contrast with Nazi Germany, and consisted of large-scale public works such as those undertaken by the Tennessee Valley Authority. As a response to the 'Great Slump', Roosevelt's New Deal marked the dawn of 'big government' for the western democracies.

The New Deal of the 1990s in the UK, however, has been born in different conditions. It follows an era of Thatcherism in which New Labour now seeks to steer a course between neo-liberal market-led approaches and Keynesian macro-economic expansionism (the concept of the Third Way which we have referred to in Chapter 1). The New Deal in the 1990s, while primarily designed to take people off welfare and into jobs, also focuses on personal responsibility and employability so that individuals can enter and progress within flexible labour markets. We will examine these assumptions later in the chapter.

The New Deal occupies this pivotal position in New Labour's political agenda because it articulates and connects a number of key political themes: a traditional ethical opposition to unemployment; a commitment to social cohesion and social inclusion; the promotion of active labour markets and 'employability' in response to the challenge of globalization and a reduction in the welfare budget.

Beyond these broad political considerations, there are very important practical reasons for the high profile of Welfare to Work strategies. The scale of welfare expenditure inherited from the Conservatives was seen to be unsustainable, particularly in the light of New Labour's commitment not to increase direct taxation. Spending on welfare had risen between 1979 and 1997 from 49 per cent to 61 per cent of total government expenditure (Kypri, 1998). By the late 1990s, New Labour had inherited an enormous social and economic problem (DSS, 1997; Labour Party, 1996e):

- workless households had doubled since 1979 from 1 in 10 to 1 in 5;
- five million people of working age were not in employment and 1 million had not worked since leaving school;
- the highest rates of unemployment were to be found in the 18–24-year-olds age group;
- 26 per cent of this age group – an estimated 250,000 – were categorized as long-term unemployed;
- 50 per cent of this age group did not have a qualification equivalent to or above NVQ 2.

New Labour dubbed these marginalized groups 'the lost generation' since they were seen as being left behind by both the labour market and by the education and training system (Labour Party, 1996e, 1996f). New Labour's approach to this group steered a course between Old Labour's belief in the cushion of the benefits system and the Conservative belief in the power of markets. New Labour is imposing a stricter benefit programme regime than that left by the Conservatives, while, at the same time, promoting a 'right to work' ethic (Finn, 1998). The Conservatives had accepted high levels of unemployment because of their commitment to market forces and also because of ideological reservations about extending the employment role of the state. The New Deal concept, seen from the position of the market-oriented Right, suggests a statutory right to work and a government role of 'employer of last resort' (Finn, 1997). However, this is an over-interpretation of New Labour's approach. It does not currently subscribe to a Keynesian concept of the state which acts to increase the supply of jobs in the public sector. Rather, it believes the state should play a central role through the processes of 'joined up government' to get people into jobs, to promote employability and, at the same time, to tackle poverty and to cement social cohesion (Mulgan, 1998; Oppenheim, 1998).

The 'Welfare to Work' strategy was developed during the period 1993–1996. Arising out of the Labour Party's Economic Policy Commission, a series of documents emerged which stressed the need to develop employability, modernize the welfare state and to invest in education, training and skills (Labour Party, 1995a, 1995b, 1996a, 1996c, 1996d). In the Shadow Budget of November 1995, New Labour outlined the elements of a programme aimed at the 18–25-year-old age group and financed through the windfall tax on the excess profits of the privatized utilities.

Like many other aspects of New Labour's education and training strategy, the New Deal represents both continuity and break with the past administration. On the one hand, Welfare to Work and, more specifically, the New Deal is seen wholly as an initiative of the New Labour Government (Educa, 1998). It is promoted as being different from previous initiatives because of its emphasis on one-to-one help, high quality education and training and follow-through, elements which have been lacking in previous initiatives to tackle youth unemployment (Blunkett, 1997; Employment

Service, 1998a). Moreover, New Labour wants to see the role of the Employment Service transformed so that it moves from policing the benefit system to advocacy on behalf of claimants seeking work. On the other hand, the strict benefit regime of the New Deal is seen by some as representing continuity with the past policy of the Conservatives (Finn, 1997).

The operation of the New Deal

The New Deal sprang to life as a government programme in the July 1997 budget, when the Chancellor, Gordon Brown, announced a total of £3.5 billion generated from a windfall tax to be spent on this programme over the lifetime of this Parliament. This represents a huge investment in tackling long-term unemployment and is the cornerstone of New Labour's social inclusion strategy for this Parliament. However, some critics of the New Deal have argued that the scheme does not represent value for money, with each placement estimated to cost over £11,000 (Green, 1998). The Government's response has been that the actual *per capita* costs of the New Deal are much lower if fully calculated over time (DfEE, 1998e).

By 1998, the New Deal for the long-term unemployed had developed two variants – the 18–24 New Deal and the 25 Plus New Deal. It may have been New Labour's long-term plan to spread the New Deal to groups other than young people, but the 25 Plus New Deal happened quickly largely because of a dramatic fall in the numbers of eligible 18–24-year-olds – from 250,000 in 1997 to about 150,000 at the beginning of 1998.

The New Deal can be regarded as an evolutionary policy process based on pilots, national programmes and an ever-expanding focus. Operating since January 1998 in 12 pathfinder areas, the New Deal for young unemployed people was introduced nationally in April 1998. This has been followed by national programmes and new initiatives for different groups such as lone parents and the disabled. The New Deal which started life with a quite specific focus on 18–24-year-olds has been taking on a wider political symbolism – there is talk of 'new deals' for different parts of society including consumers and motorists. This could be likened to the 'charters' metaphor used by the last Conservative Government. A key issue is whether the New Deal is simply a temporary and remedial policy to reduce levels of unemployment for these groups, or whether it will continue to evolve to become a permanent part of the political landscape and, in doing so, change the original meaning of the term.

18–24 New Deal

The first priority of the New Deal is to help young people to gain access to employment. It also delivers a guaranteed opportunity for employment, education or training for all young people between 18 and 24 who have been out of work and claiming the Job Seeker's Allowance continuously for over six months. The 18–24 New Deal will offer a total of 197,000 places during 1998–99.

The New Deal for 18–24-year-olds consists of three processes: the 'Gateway', the 'four Options' and the 'follow-through strategy'. The Gateway is an assessment and advisory process lasting up to 16 weeks and involving help with jobsearch, careers advice and guidance and preparation for the four Options of employment, full-time education and training, a place on the Environmental Taskforce or work in the voluntary sector. The primary focus of the Gateway is to refer jobseekers straight into non-subsidized jobs. Initial evidence, based on those who left the New Deal Gateway in 1998, suggests that just under half are doing this (DfEE, 1999c). The second part of the process relates to those who have not succeeded in gaining non-subsidized jobs. These young people are offered one of the four New Deal Options. These comprise:

- *an Employment Option:* this consists of a subsidized job with an employer who receives £60 per New Deal client per week for six months for jobs involving 30 hours a week; there is guaranteed training for one day a week and £750 available towards the cost of this training;
- *an Environmental Task Force Option:* consists of six months' work on tasks designed to improve the environment; participants receive a weekly allowance of benefit, or a wage; guaranteed training for one day per week and £750 is available for this training;
- *a Voluntary Sector Option:* consists of 6 months' work on tasks designed to improve the environment; participants receive a weekly allowance of benefit or a wage; guaranteed training for one day per week and £750 available for this training;
- *a Full-time Education and Training Option:* this lasts up to one year with payment of benefits only; education and training is mainly to Level 2 but can go beyond this if it is seen to improve employability.

However, the Prime Minister has stressed that there is no 'fifth Option of an inactive life on benefit' (Blair, 1997). If claimants reject any of the four Options without 'good cause', they will be subject to the sanctions of the 'strict benefits system'. A first refusal will result in a two-week benefit sanction and a second refusal, a four-week sanction.

The third part of the New Deal process is the 'follow-through strategy' which aims to support New Deal clients towards the goal of finding and sustaining work once they have completed one of the Options. If they have not succeeded in finding work, they are offered further support by their Employment Service personal adviser and will, if need be, re-enter the Gateway. The Gateway part of the 18–24 New Deal, therefore, reflects New Labour's approach of 'joined up government' as different agencies collaborate to support young people's needs around drugs, homelessness and debt.

The figures currently available on New Deal participation in the four Options for 1998 show that 28 per cent went into subsidized jobs, 52 per cent into full-time education and training and 10 per cent respectively to the voluntary sector and Environmental Task Force. The numbers entering the full-time education and training option appear well ahead of planning assumptions for the New Deal (Bivand, 1998).

The 25 Plus New Deal

Following the 18–24 New Deal is the 25 Plus New Deal. This aspect of the programme is more experimental. Unlike the 18–24 New Deal, the 25 Plus New Deal is not compulsory (except in the 25 Plus pilot areas). However, briefing documents state that there will be no alternative of remaining on benefit while taking no active steps to find work (Employment Service, 1998b). Launched in June 1998, the initiative was targeted at 10,000 adults. A total of £480 million has been allocated to this initiative. By the end of 1998, there were 70,000 places on offer and these are meant to use the same partnership structures and momentum built up by the 18–24 New Deal (Employment Service, 1998b).

On the other hand, there will be pilots for the 25 Plus New Deal in 28 areas, providing places for 90,000 people. With a budget of £129 million, the 25 Plus New Deal pilots will test out the effectiveness of different approaches to helping the long-term unemployed in this age group (DfEE, 1998g). The partnership approaches will be broadly the same as for the 18–24 age group, though the Government aims to increase the involvement and commitment of the private sector and has decided that one third of the pilot areas should be put out to competitive tender for private sector organizations.

Adults over 25 who have been unemployed for more than two years will be offered New Deal Options, though there are conditions under which those who been out of work for less than two years can enter the programme (DfEE, 1998h). The aim of the initiative is to 'remove barriers to unemployment; to combat employer prejudice, which will be greater for this older and longer-term unemployed group; to increase their motivation and restore self-confidence; and, where necessary to increase their employability' (Employment Service, 1998b). There are two Options – subsidized employment (£75 allowance per week but with no education and training) and the opportunity to study for up to one year while remaining on the Job Seeker's Allowance. There is also support to get a job if the participant is ready. The 25 Plus New Deal is aimed, however, at providing participants with an individual package from a combination of work-based training, work experience placement, voluntary sector and self-employment (AoC, 1998a).

Commentators argue that the 25 Plus New Deal is minimal compared with the 18–24 New Deal; it has a slimmer Gateway (AoC, 1998a), fewer Options and far less money than the 18–24 New Deal (Unemployment

Unit, 1998a). In the further education sector, concerns have also been expressed about restrictions on Level 3 study and the need for the same quality of Gateway as that provided in the 18–24 New Deal (AoC, 1998b). Ministers have responded by stating that a total of £480 million has been invested and that there will be an initial Gateway of advice and guidance – mostly jobsearch activities with Employment Service advisers (DfEE, 1998g). In areas of high unemployment, the 25 Plus New Deal will be reinforced by 'Intermediate Labour Market' projects in the prototype Employment Zones, which will allow partnerships to 'lever in' other funds from other sources (Smith, 1998).

Delivery of the New Deal

The steering of the New Deal takes place at ministerial level and is led by the Rt Hon Andrew Smith (Minister of State for Education and Employment); there is also a New Deal Task Group and a Cabinet Committee. The backbone of New Deal delivery, however, is local partnerships which try to reflect local contexts. In some areas the lead role is taken by the Employment Service; in others strategic partnerships are formed. The Government supports a varied and locally relevant approach and does not believe that the Employment Service should try to work on its own. Moreover, there is a recognition that other agencies have experience in working with young people with multiple problems of homelessness, drug dependency and debt (Smith, 1998). In this respect, there has been some success achieved through the Foyer Federation, which has about 80 units across the UK and intends over the next five years to expand this to a total of 440 providing 20,000 bed spaces (Foyer Federation, 1998). Foyers combine the offer of accommodation, training and support for young people (16–25) experiencing multiple problems of homelessness, unemployment and, in particular, for those leaving care.

Getting the initial operational structure correct is crucial for the image of the New Deal. The way it operates in its initial guidance phases will prove very important in persuading clients that the New Deal is intended to be different from earlier schemes for the unemployed and to remind people of its emphasis on quality placements, entitlement to training and access to qualifications.

Analysing dimensions of the New Deal

Performance of the 18–24 New Deal

The performance of the 18–24 New Deal in its first nine months since April 1998 has been impressive:

- the New Deal for 18–24-year-olds is large-scale with 170,000 young people having entered the Gateway – a majority of the eligible age group (DfEE, 1998i);
- 40,000 have already left the programme, the majority having moved into regular employment or other types of non-New Deal education and training; about 10 per cent have moved into other types of benefit and a quarter are still classified as 'destination unknown', most of whom are presumed to have moved into jobs (Unemployment Unit, 1998a);
- a number of large companies have signed up to the New Deal (DfEE, 1998j) – the current number of employers totals 29,000, offering almost 50,000 jobs (Unemployment Unit, 1998a);
- surveys of initial client perceptions have been found to be broadly positive: many were pleasantly surprised by the helpfulness of advisers and feelings of empowerment (Nigel Blagg Associates, 1998).

There are, however, a number of teething problems. These include slow progress of many New Dealers through the Gateway. At the beginning of 1999, of the 127,000 still participating in the New Deal, 97,000 were still on the Gateway and 28,000 were on an Option. There may be several reasons for this slow movement, including the lack of preparedness of many New Dealers to be able to move on to the next stage and the fact that Employment Service staff are trying hard not to place their clients into unsuitable jobs or Options (Unemployment Unit, 1998a). On the other hand, the process may also be a reflection of a variation in partnership or Employment Service performance. Recent figures show that some of the worst unemployment areas have achieved job entry rates that outstrip the more economically buoyant areas (Unemployment Unit, 1998b). Related to this is the emerging problem of lack of preparedness of many New Dealers for the Options, in particular the Full-Time Education and Training Option. Colleges have reported a significant proportion of New Dealers not turning up for initial interviews and failing to regularly attend education courses.[1]

Despite these problems, the programme can be seen to have made a promising start (Educa, 1998). As we have noted, the primary aim of the New Deal is to get young people off welfare and into work. So far about one quarter of those joining the New Deal have gone into subsidized or non-subsidized jobs. Many of those remaining within the programme may also follow this path but it is too early to tell. A more accurate picture of how the New Deal is performing overall is likely to emerge after about a year of operation as the programme matures and New Dealers leave the various Options. There are a number of factors laid out below which we feel might affect the outcome of the New Deal in the future and which may well prove decisive in whether it is eventually seen as a success.

Young people's attitudes and perceptions

Young people's perceptions of the New Deal and how it relates to their lives will be an important factor in determining the success of an initiative which places such an emphasis on personal responsibility and employability. So who are New Deal clients? They are largely male; often from minority ethnic groups; they tend to live in inner city areas or estates and many suffer the multiple disadvantages of unemployment, coupled with insecure housing and a record of offending or drug, alcohol and substance abuse (London TEC Council, 1997).

Various surveys of the attitudes of young people towards the New Deal have unearthed a complex picture which presents this initiative with a significant challenge (London TEC Council, 1997; Case and Atkins, 1998; Nigel Blagg Associates, 1998). Clients are usually pleasantly surprised by what the New Deal has to offer once they have had the Options explained to them, though they believe that the New Deal must lead to a worthwhile job or become a stepping stone to self-employment. Surveys also found that there is a reluctance among young people to travel beyond the home area and that peer attitudes are important, including the views of family members.

These attitude surveys suggest that young people can be won over to the New Deal, but they also pose questions as to whether a significant section of young people can be retained by the initiative. Much will depend on the quality of education and training, the personal support that is offered, including financial support for travel and, of course, the prospect of a reasonable job as an end-point. In this respect, the New Deal has yet to pass its most severe test in the eyes of young people, though initial signs are promising. The surveys suggest that for New Deal to win the battle of perceptions, it has to be seen as a 'Fair Deal' and not a 'Raw Deal' (Youthaid et al, 1997).

Race and ethnic monitoring

A particular challenge lies with getting black young people into the labour market. The unemployment rate for African Caribbeans is 34 per cent, compared to 13 per cent for all 18–24-year-olds, and a recent report has shown that racial discrimination remains a major factor in denying young people access to employment and training opportunities (Youthaid et al, 1997). Moreover, evidence from recent surveys also shows that while black people are more likely to complete their training, they are less likely to obtain a job or a qualification. This means that there will have to be ethnic monitoring of the New Deal, in particular to see if there is a disproportionate imbalance within the Employment Option. Initial monitoring statistics, collated towards the end of 1998, suggest that ethnic minorities are more likely to be in the Gateway and leave for unknown destinations than whites. They were almost equally as likely as whites to be in an unsubsidized job, though less likely to be on an Employment Option (Unemployment Unit, 1998a).

The problem of the 'revolving door'

A major problem facing the New Deal is the legacy of past schemes for the unemployed and what has been referred to as the 'revolving door' of recycling the unemployed through short-term placements (Finn, 1998). This legacy, highlighted in recent attitude surveys, means that it is incumbent on the New Deal to provide jobs with good quality training and work experience if the younger unemployed are going to escape the low-skill short duration jobs they normally get.

The image of the New Deal will, however, be created not only within the scheme itself but also by the way it is perceived externally in the wider labour market. The official publicity of the New Deal has been at pains to stress the features that make the New Deal different from previous schemes. These include one-to-one help from a personal adviser, access to a range of specialist help to tackle the barriers to unemployment and good quality work and training (Employment Service, 1997).

However, several commentators have pointed to the New Deal reproducing features of previous training and employment schemes, notably the creation of a stricter benefit regime (Finn, 1997). Some have expressed doubts as to whether the Employment Service has the capacity to work in partnership and to transform its role from benefit policing to advocacy. (Donnelly, 1997a). The threat of the 'revolving door' syndrome has raised its head with evidence from recent research that temporary part-time jobs are not working well as routes into full-time and permanent jobs (Nimmo, 1997).

As we have seen from client attitude surveys, responses to the experience of the Gateway have been largely positive. The critics of the New Deal, however, tend to focus not on the initial process (notably the Gateway) but on some of the programme's underlying assumptions about the labour market and the connection within the scheme between education, training and employment.

Employers, the labour market and the New Deal

With the economy possibly on the turn, an important issue will be the role and behaviour of employers. A number of large employers signed up to the New Deal, including leading high street names such as Tesco, Sainsbury's, Marks & Spencer and Dixons. The Government's advertising campaign to launch the New Deal appealed to employers to become part of a growing movement of those in the business community wanting to offer opportunities to young people. So far, there is no evidence of a shortage of placements. In fact, employers who have signed up for the New Deal are wondering where the applicants are, due to the slow movement out of the Gateway (Unemployment Unit, 1998b).

The fear of 'substitutionism' and the displacement of existing employees or of future recruits remains a lingering problem, though there is not much evidence of this at present. Moreover, in the 25 Plus New Deal, employers must sign a pledge that they will not engage in substitutionism practices. The real problem remains making New Dealers attractive to employers. The number of young people eligible for the New Deal in mid-1997 dropped to 150,000. This is the lowest figure since the late 1980s and the group that remains is the least employable and the most likely to suffer multiple barriers to work (Convery, 1998).

The most important issue for these New Dealers is offering intensive help and overcoming employer prejudice. The London TEC Council reported that many employers are reluctant to take on young people, regardless of level of subsidy, who have not got the right attitude, who lack numeracy and basic literacy skills and who might be ex-offenders or have drug problems (London TEC Council, 1997). Employers' views of this group of young people have been found to be generally negative – they tend to think that young people are sceptical about the programmes currently available to them, have high expectations of jobs and of salaries and have little understanding of the needs of employers or their own skill and training needs (London TEC Council, 1997).

It is clear that the success of the New Deal depends on a range of factors. The Government regards the central issue as one of individual attitude and employability. In this context, the major aim of the New Deal is to help clients to overcome multiple barriers to work, to fill existing jobs and then to retain them. For the critics, this is only half the picture. They point to the need for the labour market to create a steady supply of jobs, to offer decent levels of pay and opportunities for progression. It is possible to envisage a situation where the New Deal may experience initial success at the level of the individual client, but experience failure at the level of the economy.

The economy and the New Deal

New Labour's underlying economic assumption behind the New Deal was that it could succeed in an economy with flexible labour markets, relatively low wages and a sustainable growth rate. Professor Richard Layard, a labour market economist from the London School of Economics, regarded by some as the 'theoretical father' of the New Deal, has asserted that the quality of those seeking jobs plays an important factor in the demand for labour. Reflecting on the absence of long-term unemployment in Sweden, those advising New Labour have argued that this is the result of the combined effect of making the long-term unemployed more attractive to employers and the withdrawal of benefits after 15 months of unemployment (Layard, 1995). One could argue that New Labour's inspiration for its strict benefit regime in the New Deal, therefore, is not the British Conservatives but the Swedish Social Democrats.

Other economists have taken issue with Layard's active labour market theory. Some suggest that their assumed effects are overblown (Robinson,

1998a). The main line of criticism is that active labour market strategies may be plausible in the case of the relatively low-paid service sector, which has a high turnover of staff and where decisions to take on labour at a time of economic expansion may be significantly affected by the condition of the supply of labour.[2] However, the argument is less applicable to the manufacturing sector, where there is a demand for skills at a higher level than those likely to be provided by the New Deal and where demand is regulated by underlying structural factors, such as the lack of employer demand, and wider economic factors, such as export demand and the exchange rate.

This brings us to a crucial question about the course of the economy in the near future. Predictions of a recession and the negative effects this will have upon the New Deal appear regularly in the press. The fact is that the New Deal is a supply-side strategy which, in the end, depends upon employers' demand for labour. Layard has argued that greater levels of employability create their own momentum. If Layard is correct, a slow-down in economic growth of between 0.5 and 1 per cent (a relatively soft landing for the economy), may not significantly affect the demand for jobs, particularly if the service sector remains relatively buoyant.

However, if Layard's theory about employability creating employer demand for jobs is overstated and if the economy actually goes into recession, there could be severe problems for the New Deal in the medium term. First, fewer New Dealers will leave the Gateway and go straight to unsubsidized jobs and more will enter the four Options. Of these, the subsidized Employment Option will further decrease in size and more clients will have to enter the three remaining Options. Moreover, when New Dealers come to leave the programme, it is likely that fewer of them will progress into stable employment. In this context, New Labour might have to review seriously the Education and Training Option so that it becomes more substantial than it currently is. There is some evidence that this Option has grown more than initially envisaged. This might be seen as changing the fundamental emphasis of the New Deal from employment with a focus on jobs to employability with a focus on education and training.

Further education and the role of education and training in the New Deal

In the light of the growing importance of education and training within the New Deal and the proportion of New Dealers now entering the Full-Time Education and Training Option, a great deal of responsibility for the success of the programme lies with further education colleges and other training providers. The recognition of the role of education in employability is seen as a radical element of the New Deal (Donnelly, 1997a).

The relationship between the New Deal and further education colleges is, therefore, an important barometer of the New Deal's education and training capacity and its ability to fulfil its radical promise. Further education colleges have become closely involved in the formation of local strategic partnerships and are the most likely providers of the education and training aspects of the New Deal (Kypri, 1998). However, in associating themselves with the New Deal initiative in these ways, colleges have encountered a number of problems and in particular in relation to limits of level of qualification and level of funding (Donnelly, 1997a; Jupp and Scribbens, 1998).

First, in responding to the statistic that over 50 per cent of the age group did not have a qualification up to Level 2, New Labour decided that qualification to this level should be a priority. However, further education colleges were already catering for unemployed learners on Job Seeker's Allowance and some of these students were undertaking Access and Level 3 courses. It was possible, therefore, that in order to qualify for the New Deal they might have to leave these higher level courses. Not only would this be disruptive to these individual learners, it would be in direct contradiction to the Kennedy Report which called for 'a lifetime entitlement to education up to Level 3, which is free for young people and those who are socially and economically deprived' (Kennedy, 1997: 13). When lobbied by representatives of further education colleges, the Rt Hon Andrew Smith (Minister of State) stated that Level 3 courses could be seen as part of the New Deal 'if there is a clear path to employment and employability' (Jupp and Scribbens, 1998). Jupp and Scribbens argue that the whole range of Schedule 2 QCA approved courses should be open to New Dealers without this condition. Moreover, they are concerned that the message from the Minister about New Dealers' eligibility for Level 3 courses has not been getting through to the Employment Service, which advises clients, and that this gives the wrong message about the importance of upskilling.

The second major problem with the New Deal for further education colleges is the level of funding they receive. Indicative funding for these learners is less than that received for learners funded at FEFC rates and colleges also have to provide more hours of tuition and support. Colleges have been keen to become involved in the New Deal and many feel that they have been forced to bid for New Deal provision at low rates in order not to be excluded from the programme. As a result they are being compelled to cross-subsidize New Deal students by a reduction of service to other students. One college has calculated that it will stand to lose over £500,000 by co-operating with the New Deal in 1998 (Jupp and Scribbens, 1998).

The problem of the relationship between further education colleges and the New Deal may lie not only with the nature of the New Deal funding and qualification rules but also with the lack of flexibility of college provision. A sudden leap in the numbers entering the Education and Training Option in September has been linked to the start of the academic year (Unemployment Unit, 1998b). This arouses suspicion that colleges might have closed their doors to new recruits until next September. Colleges, on the other hand, will argue that insufficient funding forces them to infill New Dealers into courses. Moreover, there is currently an inherent lack of flexibility in the qualifications system which has yet to move to the type of credit accumulation and transfer system required to support more flexible learning opportunities.

Despite these problems, further education colleges are becoming centrally involved in local partnerships and are adapting their provision to provide customized induction programmes, jobsearch skills, key skills and monitoring systems, as well as working closely with the Employment Service (Beverley, 1998). These changes, although in some cases posing considerable challenges for colleges, will also benefit other students and will improve the capacity of colleges to widen participation (Beales, 1998).

The benefit system, sanctions and incentives to work

A central assumption of the New Deal is that the programme will provide sufficient incentive to attract the young unemployed. However, it is not yet clear whether the tax, benefits and wages system is sufficiently developed to provide sustainable incentives for some groups to take up employment and to remain within work

The main problem is what has been termed the unemployment and benefit poverty trap. This broadly describes a situation in which some of those out of work would be little better off financially in work because of the loss of their benefits and because of the low wages they would receive in employment. This problem is not simply associated with low pay, but also with an inflexible benefit system. For example, there are many part-time jobs available, but the unemployed cannot take advantage of this type of work because of the risk of a disproportionate loss of benefit. This has been described as the 'flexible labour market, inflexible benefit system' (Nimmo, 1997).

The Unemployment Unit, with extensive experience of working with the unemployed, has identified four obstacles to individuals changing their circumstances: bureaucratic hassle, interruption of income, uncertainty over the future level of income and the risk to future benefit entitlement. It argues that the answer is not to reduce benefits for those out of work, because the extreme tightness of family budgets deters people from the risk of taking a job. Finding a job, for example, may mean facing the prospect of attracting demands from creditors. For many it is easier to sink into the world of the black economy and various forms of petty crime. Young people report this process could be exacerbated by a regime of tighter sanctions (London TEC Council, 1997). The Unemployment Unit argues for a radical reform and integration of the tax/benefit system, possibly along the lines of the Australian model, which allows individuals to be in receipt of benefit right up to the point where they reach two-thirds of average earnings. This encourages them to take up part-time work.

The other issue for the New Deal concerns the type of sanctions young people face if they refuse to become involved in unemployment programmes. The

New Deal programme is draconian in this respect (Finn, 1997, 1998). Interestingly, research suggests that there is support amongst the unemployed for sanctions, but nearly all feel that the process they are forced to go through is degrading and there are many who resent having been wrongly treated (Donnelly, 1997b). Moreover, research suggests that the New Deal process has to become significantly less bureaucratic and more user-friendly and there is some initial evidence that the New Deal is gaining a reputation among some unemployed for being different from the Job Seeker's Allowance, though the image of the Job Seeker's Allowance looms large (Case and Atkins, 1998).

It is difficult not to conclude that the New Deal requires both a cultural and a structural 'revolution' in the benefit system if it is to provide a sustainable ladder out of benefit and into work. New Labour is having to work with a benefits machinery inherited from the Conservatives and presently much is being done to reform the benefits system (eg Working Families Tax Credits and Child Care Credits). Moreover, certain groups can now study full-time without loss of benefits. But the process of reorganizing the relationship between benefits, taxes and wages will have to go much further if the Government wants to provide marginalized groups with genuine incentives rather than simply forcing them to work.

New Deal and challenges for New Labour

New Deal is a flagship programme for New Labour, not only because of its high profile in the 1997 general election campaign, but because it brings together key themes of the New Labour political and ideological agenda: a crusade against unemployment, the concepts of personal employability and social inclusion and connections between welfare reform and low taxation.

In economic terms, the New Deal is a big programme consisting of over £3.5 billion to be spent this Parliament. The various types of New Deal initiative reflect a deep-seated commitment on behalf of the Government to tackle the issue of long-term unemployment and social marginalization which it sees as detrimental to both the unemployed and to society at large. Much of the evidence gleaned so far suggests that the New Deal has got off to a promising start. The initial client surveys have been largely positive and there is enthusiasm among the partnerships and providers to see things work despite some early difficulties, most notably in the further education sector, and the variability of performance of different geographical areas.

There are significant challenges ahead as the New Deal programme expands and as the economy slows down. It is likely to become much more difficult to keep up the supply of placements, to propel New Dealers from the Gateway into non-subsidized jobs and to provide sustainable employment at the end of the various Options. However, these are the criteria against which the New Deal is likely to be judged in the long term. New Labour should also take note of the survey of young people's attitudes.

Young people appear to agree with a tough approach to the workshy, providing that those in programmes are treated decently and that those who complete the programme are offered reasonable employment opportunities.

So how should the New Deal be evaluated at this point in time? We will initially suggest a two-dimensional approach – an evaluation at the level of the individual and an evaluation at the level of the education, training, welfare and labour market system. The New Deal is potentially radical from the individual perspective. It emphasizes the supportive ongoing personal relationship between the adviser and the client, the role of the Gateway and the guidance process and a multi-agency approach tackling the often complex and multi-dimensional problems experienced by many of the young long-term unemployed. Moreover, education and training are meant to be an integral part of the New Deal. This is a new type of policy emphasis and is broadly welcomed.

In the longer term, it is system issues which are likely to give cause for concern. New Labour has argued that fiscal stability and the end of 'boom and bust' economics will provide the climate for employment growth (Labour Party, 1995a). However, a government preoccupation with keeping inflation at a low level, combined with the effects of the global economic crisis, could result in a 'hard landing' for the economy. If the economy does enter a full-blooded recession, the New Deal may 'revert to type' and become like its predecessors – keeping down the unemployment figures rather than marking a transition from benefit to work. Faced with such a prospect, the Government might be forced to take more interventionist measures to boost public investment and to increase the supply of public sector jobs. The Chancellor's £50 billion earmarked for investment in health, education, housing and transport might have even more significance than originally thought. In the first instance, calls have been made for more interventionist and holistic economic planning in the Employment Zones (Finn, 1997).

As the Unemployment Unit argues, we have flexible labour markets but an inflexible tax/benefit system. The unemployed are not always able to take full advantage of the supply of part-time jobs because they fear loss of benefit. While there is promise of tax/benefit reforms, these reforms still appear to be some way off. Yet there is an urgent need to produce a more tapered tax system with a lower starting rate (eg 10 per cent) and to allow the retention of more benefit while in work. If, on the other hand, New Labour does not want to be seen to be subsidizing poverty pay, then it has to develop other measures in relation to low pay.

Given the centrality of education and training to employability, the New Deal has to be totally unambiguous about offering education and training opportunities. This has not been the case so far. The Level 3 capping issue, the low funding rate offered to further education colleges and the retention of the 16-hour rule have resulted in mixed messages. New Labour has to provide a clear message that education makes a difference by fully adopting the

Kennedy (1997) agenda on widening participation.

In conclusion, the New Deal is a serious programme designed to address unemployment and marginalization for a vulnerable group of people. For this reason it needs and deserves to work. Moreover, there appears to be a great deal of goodwill towards the programme. The immediate political test for the New Deal lies with the 18–24-year-old variant because of its high profile. The 25 Plus New Deal may, however, in the longer term be more significant in reshaping the relationship between government and labour markets. In reaching a judgement about how to assess the New Deal, we will argue that both programmes will face four tests:

1. achieving an image which is different from early programmes for the unemployed;
2. being effective in moving New Dealers through the Gateway into non-subsidized jobs;
3. developing effective Options which adequately prepare New Dealers to move into the labour market;
4. developing sustainable employment rather than the emergence of the 'revolving door'.

New Labour appears to have passed the first test and to have been partially successful in terms of the second, with regards to the 18–24 New Deal. The remaining two tests are far more difficult to achieve and only time will tell whether the New Deal strategy will be successful in these areas. To achieve this will depend not only on the operation of the New Deal, which has to date been largely focused around the Gateway, but also on relationships between education and training and the wider economy. The early signs are promising, but the challenges ahead are daunting both in terms of reaching the 'harder to get' sections of the population and coping with an economy which, by 1999, might have slowed significantly or could be in recession.

We would like to conclude this chapter on a speculative note, not only with regard to judgements on the performance of the New Deal, but also in relation to its underlying assumptions. The New Deal concept is premised on the combined effects of flexible labour markets and active government intervention to promote employability. If Professor Layard is correct in his assumptions, then the New Deal will work, at least in the short term. If, on the other hand, employers in the UK continue with their propensity not to invest in skills development and to seek cost-cutting routes to competitiveness (see Chapter 4), then the initial momentum of the New Deal may not be sustainable. Not enough jobs will be created and those that are will tend to be low skill. It would be a great pity to see the programme initially succeed at the level of many individual New Dealers and some companies, only to be let down by the wider employment, education and training system of which it is only a part.

If New Labour wants the New Deal to work in the long run, it may have to look more closely at the underlying system barriers which not only exclude people from work but which can lock them into low-skill jobs. In terms of the weak and strong framework analysis elaborated in Chapter 7, the New Deal is a paradox. It employs a strong approach to collaboration to break the cycle of long-term unemployment, but it may be comparatively weak in producing the kind of strong partnerships for sustained skill development and sustainable employment. These themes are taken up further in Chapter 4.

Notes

1 Seminar 'New Deal: One Year On' Institute of Education, University of London, 3 February 1999.
2 The Dixons Group may typify the kind of employer Layard has in mind. Dixons has 900 outlets and is seeking to create 3,000 new jobs nationwide. It is looking for recruits among the unemployed who have 'commitment, honesty and integrity' (Educa, 1998: 5).

4

Skills, Training and the World of Work

The Conservative legacy

The development of skills in the population as a whole is seen by New Labour as central to economic competitiveness in an era of rapid technological change. 'It is only by investing for the future, employing the skills and talents of all members of our society, and facing up to the challenges of an increasingly competitive global economy, that Britain can prosper into the 21st century' (Labour Party, 1995a). However, compared to other advanced industrial countries, the UK is widely recognized to suffer from a skills gap (CBI, 1989; DTI, 1994; DfEE, 1998k). Closing the skills gap and developing skills for the future is, therefore, a huge challenge for a government that places so much political emphasis on the role of education and training in producing the basis of future prosperity. Because of the centrality of these themes, this chapter focuses on New Labour's approach to training and skill development within the world of work.

The Conservative legacy handed down to the Labour Government in the area of skills and the world of work can be seen to consist of four 'system' problems – the skills gap; low employer demand for skills; a marketized and mixed education and training system; and the effects of long-term unemployment and the uneven distribution of education and training opportunities.

International comparative analysis has suggested that the skills gap between the UK and competitor countries is most severe at intermediate level, which includes craft, technician and associate professional occupations (Steedman and Green 1997; DfEE, 1998k). The interpretation of this skills gap has focused on the marginal role of the work-based route within the UK and the low status of vocational qualifications (Richardson *et al*, 1995), the implications of which are explored later in the chapter.

Low employer demand for skill is an underlying structural problem of the vocational education and training (VET) system and also a legacy of the Conservative era. Previously analysed as an aspect of the 'low skills equilibrium' (Finegold and Soskise, 1988), low demand for skills is the result of the options open to employers within the UK system to adopt low-cost/low price competitiveness strategies. These include focusing on a standardized range of products, shedding costs rather than investing in skills, contracting out and employing casual labour and, where necessary, poaching skilled labour (Keep and Mayhew, 1997). The syndrome of low-skill demand does not necessarily mean that British employers invest less in skills than their competitors (Robinson, 1998b), but that they tend to do so to meet short-term needs rather than using skills investment as part of an overall strategy of labour market utilization for long-term competitive advantage.

The third aspect of the legacy inherited by New Labour, and the direct result of Conservative policy, was the development of a marketized and mixed initial post-compulsory education and training system.[1] The early 1990s saw concerted efforts to establish a deregulated and competitive education and training market based on employer-led organizations, outcome-related qualifications and funding and training credits (Hodkinson and Sparkes, 1994). The system was not only marketized but mixed – that is, it was neither predominantly school-based nor work-based (Raffe, 1992). The decline of the youth labour market gave rise to a low participation mixed system in the 1980s and then a medium-participation mixed system in the 1990s (Spours, 1995). One result of this path of development has been the continued decline of the apprenticeship system and a marginalized work-based route (Richardson and Gumbley, 1995).

The fourth aspect of the Conservative legacy was an economy which had for some time been characterized by slow growth rates and persistent levels of unemployment. This was criticized by New Labour as a massive waste of human talent and the main reason for the growth of poverty and inequality (Labour Party, 1995a). It is the association of unemployment with skills deficits that has become the distinctive hallmark of the Labour Government's strategy for this Parliament.

New Labour's approach: employability and individual skill development

As the policies of the Labour Government evolve during this Parliament, its approach to upskilling the population is based on a number of Third Way-related principles based on a belief about what governments can and cannot do. Education is seen as one of the main powers left to national governments in an increasingly globalized market economy and there is a view that this power should be exercised in such a way as to promote social justice and social cohesion. This emphasis on education in New Labour's policy hierarchy is, therefore, intimately bound up with the perceived limits of both markets and government (Plant, 1998).

Second, during the period 1993–96 and influenced by the Commission on Social Justice (1994), New Labour developed a conviction that the most effective ways of promoting skills and reducing social division was by tackling levels of literacy, long-term unemployment and providing opportunities for individual participation and skill development. The central theme of New Labour's approach to skills would be 'employability'. The newness of New Labour's approach lies in the sheer scale of the programmes and initiatives in this area and their linkages with literacy and basic skills strategies aimed at promoting social inclusion rather than promoting market competition.

Third, the role of government is seen as one of stimulating a popular demand for skills within the framework of flexible labour markets and social legislation (DfEE, 1998l). This approach is reflected in a wide range of initiatives such as Individual Learning Accounts, the University for Industry and Employee Development Schemes (DfEE, 1998a).

Finally, in moving between top-down regulation and market competition, New Labour places an emphasis on 'partnership' and 'joined-up government'. Within this approach different government agencies are required to work together around common agendas; a notable catalyst being the newly created Social Exclusion Unit. Partnerships are also initiative- and project-driven as the Government seeks to find out what can work within the dual constraints of minimum levels of regulation from the state and keeping public expenditure in check.

By 1996, New Labour's plans in relation to education and training and the world of work began to crystallize. Ideas and policies relating to working life were spread across four major documents – *A New Economic Future for Britain* (Labour Party, 1995a), *Learn as You Earn: Labour's plans for a skills revolution* (1996d), *Lifelong Learning* (1996a) and *Aiming Higher* (1996b). These documents highlighted a range of policies which appear to fall into three types – New Labour's own flagship programmes; those policies inherited from the previous government; and, third, less developed plans for more structural change within the VET system.

New Labour's 1996 document *Learn as You Earn: Labour's plans for a skills revolution*, identified four initiatives which have constituted the main thrust of policy in relation to the workplace during the first two years of government. These include 'The New Deal for 18–24-Year-Olds', 'Learn as you Earn' through Individual Learning Accounts (ILAs), and the 'University for Industry' (UfI); and 'The Right to Learn' programme for 16–17-year-olds.

The second category of policies are those inherited from the Conservatives, but which have been given a New Labour interpretation. These include Modern Apprenticeships, National Traineeships, Target 2000 (a rebranded Youth Training), Investors in People which is aimed at encouraging small enterprises to train and employee development programmes.

The third category, which is seen as longer-term because of its implications for restructuring the education and training system, includes the reform of vocational qualifications and creating a national credit framework; a review of tax incentives, grants and benefits systems with a view to encouraging education and training and the creation of regional planning structures.

New Labour's most significant policy change during the period running up to the general election was the dropping of the revised version of the training levy rebate system. To appreciate the historical significance of this policy shift it should be remembered that it was the Labour Party, during the 1960s and 1970s, that had supported the development of the 17 'tri-partite' Industrial Training Boards (ITBs) and a Comprehensive Manpower Strategy (McCarthy, 1997).

Faced with the legacy of a deregulated and marketized system and deter-mined to steer a course away from old Labour corporatism, New Labour focused on providing 'economic opportunities for all our citizens to work, train and study' (Labour Party, 1995a: 9). In this document, New Labour's strategy still hung in the balance with a call for a 'revised version of the training levy system'. By 1996, the emphasis had changed significantly. Gone were the demands that companies 'had to provide education and training for their staff'. This had been replaced by a more voluntarist approach – Individual Learning Accounts, Investors in People and the University for Industry. The reasons for the shift were both political and technical. In the context of a push for a National Minimum Wage and the adoption of the Social Charter, it was thought that any further demands on employers would prove to be politically difficult (Robinson, 1998a). Moreover, ITBs and the levy were seen to have affected only a minority of companies and sectors. With the new emphasis on flexible labour markets and reaching small and medium-sized employers, the statutory framework for employers' contribution to training was weakened and reliance placed on incentivizing the individual learner. The New Labour emphasis on social inclusion and individual responsibility did not seek to change the direction or underlying dynamics of the education and training system. Instead, as we have argued earlier, it was designed to address the negative manifestations of years of Conservative government by removing the 'tail' of underachievement and exclusion and by empowering the individual learner.

New Labour's policies in operation – a review of the first two years

The Labour Government's policies for skills development at work and beyond can be analysed in relation to four themes – policies on the work-based route for 16–21-year-olds based on Modern Apprenticeships and National Traineeships; components of the *Investing in Young People* strategy aimed at disaffected and disadvantaged 14–17-year-olds; initia-tives and programmes designed to promote social inclusion and skill improvement for the adult population; and policies to develop the training infrastructure.

New Labour and the work-based route for 16–21-year-olds

The historical marginalization of the work-based route

Work-based training has played a relatively marginal role for the younger age group in the UK compared to other European systems as 'public policy has swung to and fro between full-time and part-time routes' (Ryan, 1998: 291). The reasons for this are both historical and policy-related. The UK never established a strong and comprehensive apprenticeship system in the same way as in Germany or Austria. In the 1970s, even as apprenticeships were expanding, most young people left school and made a transition to jobs without formal training and qualifications. Under the impact of youth unemployment during the early 1980s, the Youth Training Scheme (YTS) introduced new forms of training aimed at socializing youth (Bates *et al*, 1984) and developing generic and transferable skills (Ainley and Corney, 1990). Despite the fact that at any one time more than 250,000 young people were involved in youth training programmes, the work-based route played only a minor role in improving qualifications outcomes. Moreover, during this period, apprenticeships continued to decline and, by the early 1990s, were in a state of collapse.

The marginalization of the work-based route also affected proposals for reform. Those suggesting radical change in the education and training system were ready to pronounce the work-based route a hopeless case (Finegold *et al*, 1990). It was envisaged that participation in full-time education would continue to include over 80 per cent of the cohort at 16 (CBI, 1993) and some suggested that the UK should follow the American full-time education model (Soskise, 1993). Even reformers committed to the potential of apprenticeships were sceptical of the capacity of the work-based route to deliver quality training and felt compelled to propose a system based on full-time traineeships supported by local learning co-ordination units (Evans *et al*, 1997).

Predictions of the demise of the work-based route were, however, premature. By 1995, the plateauing of participation rates in full-time education moved attention back to the potential role of the work-based route to improve levels of participation and achievement (Richardson *et al*, 1995). It was argued that under the right kind of conditions (eg those provided by reputable work-based training programmes such as Modern Apprenticeships), increasing numbers of young people would opt to be trained and qualified at work rather than in full-time education (Unwin, 1997). At the same time, it was also argued that the work-based route is better at reducing skills deficits than full-time education provision, because the training it provides is more directly related to employer needs (Steedman *et al*, 1998). This renewed interest in apprenticeship was not only confined to the UK but was part of a international search for maximizing levels of participation and improving skill formation (Lasonen and Young, 1998; OECD, 1996).

These developments and debates provided the background for New Labour's policies on the work-based route. Prior to the general election, it proposed the abolition of the Youth Training programme on the grounds that it lacked credibility among young people and did not require the achievement of a Level 2 qualification (Labour Party, 1996b). Its place would be taken by the 'Target 2000' programme which would provide at least six hours per week of study for everyone under 18 who did not have a Level 2. Moreover, employers would have an obligation to ensure that this type of study was available for all employees. New Labour also supported the principles of the Modern Apprenticeship scheme (and subsequently National Traineeships) but was concerned about its performance and its lack of breadth compared to equivalent programmes abroad (Labour Party, 1996a, 1996b).

Modern Apprenticeships and National Traineeships

Modern Apprenticeships (MAs), announced in the November 1993 Budget, are an employer-led training framework which aims to boost the number of young people entering the labour market with craft, technician and junior management skills. More specifically, MAs are designed to provide 16–19-year-olds with training leading to a Level 3 qualification rather than being based on time-serving, as was the case in the traditional apprenticeship. Each MA framework is developed by a national training organization (NTO) based on the needs of a particular industrial sector. Frameworks have now been developed across about 80 sectors, including both traditional occupations, such as engineering, and new sectors, such as retail, which did not have a history of apprenticeship. By the beginning of 1998, there were 117,000 modern apprentices in England and Wales, though this total is still less than the number of apprenticeships lost during the 1990s (Steedman *et al*, 1998).

Since their piloting and introduction in 1994, MAs have been generally regarded as a success. Employed status has been a condition for about 95 per cent of apprentices and this, together with an emphasis on Level 3 qualifications, has made them much sought after and capable of attracting some high achieving school-leavers (Unwin and Wellington, 1995). In addition, they have brought about a significant increase (about 16 per cent) in the number of establishments undertaking intermediate skill training and have increased the uptake of NVQs (Hasluck *et al*, 1997).

The early success of MAs resulted in them being emulated at Level 2. Sir Ron Dearing, in his *Review of Qualifications for 16–19-Year-Olds* (1996) and influenced by research on the problems of the work-based route (Richardson, 1998), ventured beyond his brief to propose that National Traineeships (NTs) should replace the YT programme. NTs became available from September 1997 and there are plans for their development in over 60 different sectors. NTs extend many of the principles of MAs to Level 2 training, though in a more diluted form. Employed status is desirable but not compulsory; NTs are meant to provide a progression route into MAs, though only a minority of schemes have this explicit aim, and there is a lower employer commitment to broad vocational education than in MAs.

New Labour's approach to the work-based route

New Labour's approach to the work-based route is essentially a continuation of policies inherited from the Conservatives who, in their latter years, were compelled to respond to their increasingly marginalized position. Like the Conservatives, the Labour Government recognizes that these programmes have the potential to attract young people to the work-based route and to improve qualification outputs. It is not yet clear, however, whether New Labour will evolve a distinctive approach to these programmes. The DfEE *Education and Training Agenda* (DfEE, 1997c) states that priorities will include improving access to MAs, progression between programmes and equal opportunities – which can be seen as an application of the social inclusion principle.

While there is a widespread consensus that MAs and NTs are the right course of action for the work-based route, they are not immune from wider system and negative policy effects. These may prove to be the real problem for New Labour. Despite calls to double the number of MAs in the next five years (Steedman *et al*, 1998), the factors listed below suggest that this is unlikely to happen or that the Government is prepared to employ the means to bring it about.

First, the growth of MAs in established sectors such as engineering is slowing; a process exacerbated by the economic slowdown (Maguire, 1998). Second, in those sectors such as retailing, where there is still considerable room for expansion, large companies are meeting labour market needs by recruiting casual youth labour rather than by providing full-time jobs with training (Hodgson and Spours, 1998). Sainsbury's currently employs only 300 full-time 16–19-year-olds but over 13,000 part-time (Sainsbury plc, 1998). A third factor is the potential impact of New Labour's own social inclusion policies. The New Deal for 18–24-year-olds and the development of NTs at Levels 1 and 2 may undermine the commitment of companies to further expand MAs at Level 3 (Maguire, 1998). A fourth factor is the role of Training and Enterprise Councils (TECs) in funding MAs. Locally based TECs, in contrast with the sector-based NTOs, have to respond to their own targets provided by government, to local labour market pressures and to funding constraints. These, combined with weak or variable employer demand for skills, may be preventing a co-ordinated approach to MAs across the country (Vickerstaff, 1998). These system factors – unregulated labour markets and low employer demand for skills; current policy emphasis on social inclusion and weak planning mechanisms – threaten to combine in such a way as to curtail the growth of MAs and thus undermine the road to quality in the work-based route.

Components of the Investing in Young People strategy

In the long term, the Government would like all young people not involved in full-time education to enter a progression ladder in the work-based route based on NTs and MAs. In the meantime, New Labour is putting in place a range of initiatives and provision aimed at 14–19-year-olds not fully integrated into these two routes under the umbrella of the *Investing in Young People* strategy (DfEE, 1997d). These include Target 2000, the *New Start* strategy aimed at disaffected young people from 14, *Right to Learn* legislation to encourage qualification at Level 2 for 16 and 17-year-olds and a new *Gateway for the Most Disadvantaged 16–17-Year-Olds*. Below, we briefly review some of these initiatives.

Target 2000 is a rebadged youth training programme applicable to about 10–15 per cent of the cohort. It provides training for young people who have yet reached Level 2 and to whom employers are not yet ready to make a commitment of employed status. There is, however, the possibility of progression into NTs. The Government would like to see a gradual phasing out of Target 2000 so that all those in the work-based route participate within NT and MA programmes.

New Labour has also legislated to give young people in unskilled jobs, who do not yet have a Level 2 qualification, an entitlement to receive education and training on- or off-the-job to help them attain the qualification (DfEE, 1997d). However, the onus is not on the employer to offer training but on individuals to take up their entitlement and, if need be, to take the employer to a tribunal. Under these conditions, it is anticipated that the take-up will be low (Robinson, 1998a). Moreover, it has been argued that the cut-off at 18 years and a restriction to Level 2 does not address the future skill needs of many individuals and employers (TUC, 1997).

Another aspect of its *Investing in Young People Strategy* is the proposed gateway for the most disadvantaged 16 and 17-year-olds. To be introduced in late 1999, the new gateway will be aimed at those young people who cannot immediately enter NVQ Level 2 or equivalent. Modelled on the guidance process of the New Deal for 18–24-year-olds and 17 *New Start* projects, the proposed gateway for 16 to 17-year-olds will attempt to draw those young people who suffer multiple disadvantages and have 'dropped out', back into education and training through a guidance process supported by community outreach and personal support (DfEE, 1998m).

The *Investing in Young People* strategy is another reflection of New Labour's commitment to social and education inclusion and its attempt to put in place provision for all parts of the 14–18 age group between compulsory education and the New Deal. However, we will argue that, like other aspects of New Labour's approach, such initiatives need to be supported by radical changes in the qualifications system and strong incentives for cross-institutional collaboration and greater employer involvement if they are to succeed in the longer term. These issues are pursued further in Chapters 6 and 7.

Initiatives for skills in working life

New Labour's flagship policies in this Parliament for the world of work are those most clearly associated with the aims of promoting social inclusion and lifelong learning. These initiatives are explained in some depth in Chapter 2; here we will focus briefly on their role in relation to working life and on four of them in particular – Individual Learning Accounts, the University for Industry, Investors in People and employee development programmes.

Individual Learning Accounts

Individual Learning Accounts (ILAs) occupy a special place in New Labour's plans for skills because they represent an individual demand-led approach in which the State provides a framework within which individuals then take responsibility for their future (Clough, 1998). An ILA is a savings account acting as a personal investment in learning. Some accounts may enable individuals to borrow money for their learning needs and people will be able to withdraw their own money at any time for any purpose. By the year 2000, the Government aims to develop a national framework of accounts available to everyone. In the meantime, 1 million ILAs are being subsidized by £150 million of funds from TEC reserves, some of which will be targeted at people without qualifications and in low skill jobs, people who wish to develop skills in short supply, employees in small firms and those seeking to return to work.

While the general principle of ILAs is broadly supported, there is scepticism about whether the current framework of policy will work as envisaged. Barriers to participation remain – recipients will receive £150 worth of training and but will have to contribute £25 from their own pocket, so those most in need of training may be deterred. It is likely, therefore, that most of the 1 million accounts will be opened by the skilled rather than the unskilled. The ILA may well then drift 'up-market'. This, in itself, is positive in terms of skills development in this country but could result in 'dead-weight'. The better companies and more motivated workers are more likely to become involved, whereas the less motivated companies and more marginalized workers (often those in temporary or part-time work) may not. Moreover, the banks do not seem to be interested in ILAs and even the more lucrative individual savings accounts are encountering resistance in the banking sector. It is possible, therefore, that ILAs could peter out following the end of the subsidy from TEC reserves (Clough, 1998).

For ILAs to succeed in promoting both social inclusiveness and economic competitiveness they will require consistent funding from government and also leverage on employers. In large companies, brokerage for ILAs can be provided by trades unions (Payne, 1998), but other mechanisms will have to be created for small and medium enterprises. Prior to the election, New Labour argued for changes to the tax-benefit system and declared a commitment to the Learning Bank (Labour Party, 1996d). However, as Chapter 2 points out, since the election and in government the current version of ILAs is not linked to the concept of a 'Learning Bank'. In addition, the Government has, for the time being, decided against any tax changes and has, instead, decided that incentives for training will be confined to Career Development and Small Firm Training Loans (DfEE, 1997c).

The University for Industry

The University for Industry (UfI), is the other 'flagship' initiative in which information communications technologies and guidance programmes are used together to provide greater access to education and training opportunities and, thereby, to stimulate personal demand for training (see Chapter 2 for further details of UfI).

The UfI Pathfinder Prospectus lists indicative targets of 200,000 people per year to undertake ICT programmes at Levels 1, 2 and 3; UfI programmes to be delivered to 100,000 start-up businesses and 50,000 established SMEs per year and a focus on the automative components industry, multimedia industry, environmental technology and services and distributive and retail trades (DfEE *et al*, 1998). It is envisaged that UfI will encourage benchmarking of performance and the identification of skill needs, the provision of information and advice services and the development of learning networks and services. It is planned that the UfI will be fully operational by the year 2000, and by 2002 there is a target of 2.5 million people or businesses using the UfI's services every year and 600,000 pursuing learning programmes.

At this stage, UfI still remains a largely unknown quantity. At one level, the challenges facing ILAs are also broadly applicable to UfI. Those who most need education and training opportunities will require the most support in gaining access. Unless this is addressed, the UfI risks ending up a 'high tech' opportunity for those who have already benefited most from learning. Furthermore, the impact of UfI may be limited if it does not engage organizations as well as individuals. Early evidence suggests that this will be the crux of the problem. The IPPR/UfI pilot in Sunderland succeeded in recruiting school failures, drop-outs and disadvantaged adults to study and, in particular, to draw them into IT taster courses. However, small and medium enterprises were harder to engage (Milner *et al*, 1999).

Investors in People

Investors in People (IiP) is a national standard awarded to organizations that place the development of people at the heart of their business strategy. Developed originally within the Conservatives' market-driven system, IiP was adopted by New Labour in 1996 as one of the alternatives for its revised training levy rebate system. Interestingly, IiP was not mentioned in the 1995 document *A New Economic Future for Britain*.

IiP has been a relative success in large companies and, like Modern Apprenticeships, is generally well-regarded. In 1996, 24 per cent of the workforce worked in companies with IiP, but the penetration of small and medium-sized enterprises (SMEs) was much lower. New Labour planned, therefore, to focus IiP on SMEs with measures to make the programme more accessible and to look at how purchasing of goods and services by central and local government could take account of a commitment to IiP by contractors and suppliers (Labour Party, 1996d). Since coming to power, the Labour Government has planned 12 pilots which will link small firms with large firm 'mentors' and will bring together groups of customers and suppliers, and IiP is included in the new National Learning Targets.

While progress will undoubtedly be made with some small firms, it is difficult to see how voluntarist co-operation can be sufficiently strong to offset the negative pull factors of the low-skills equilibrium, mentioned earlier in the chapter, which disproportionately affects small companies. It is likely, therefore, that IiP in its current form will have only a limited impact on skills levels.

Employee development schemes and 'Bargaining for Skills'

Another component of New Labour's strategy for skills in the workplace is employee development schemes and *Bargaining for Skills* projects. Like several other aspects of current Labour policy, they were already in place during the Conservative era. Successful employee development schemes include Unison's 'Return to Learn' and the Ford Employee Development and Assistance Programme (EDAP). Employee development schemes often involve partnerships between TECs, unions, NTOs and colleges. *Bargaining for Skills* projects, on the other hand, are union led and there are currently 10 regional projects working with 60 TECs to help trade unions to play an active role in work-based learning.

Under the new Government the role of unions in skills development has been given a high profile by the Secretary of State, the Rt Hon David Blunkett, with a total of £8 million being provided by Government between 1998 and 2001. These 45 projects can be seen as an attempt to stimulate a 'bottom-up' demand for skills. However, like many other bottom-up approaches, they will be affected by the wider economic and industrial relations context. Local economic turbulence can disrupt partnerships (eg changes in company ownership or downsizing) and these projects are not able to penetrate companies where they might be needed most, such as those with little employer commitment and casualized work.

Reform of the training infrastructure

New Labour's concept of the role of the active State in relation to employers is to provide a climate of economic stability alongside frameworks for collaboration with other providers, both nationally and locally. Currently, New Labour does not believe in compelling employers to train or in using taxation as a means of encouraging the demand for skills. Instead, it believes in providing an enabling rather than an overtly regulatory agenda.

The Government's approach to skill development and the training infra-structure revolves around a number of developments which can be divided into four main areas; first, a more planned and co-ordinated approach to skill development through National Training Organizations (NTOs), Training and Enterprise Councils (TECs) and Regional Development Agencies (RDAs); second, the establishment of a National Skills Taskforce; third, New National Learning Targets; and finally, the reform of National Vocational Qualifications (NVQs).

National Training Organizations, TECs and Regional Development Agencies

The development of a co-ordinated infrastructure to replace the complex and voluntarist, market-led system of employer-led agencies, which New Labour inherited from the previous administration, is still in its early stages of development. Its eventual shape is, as yet, not very clear, though it is likely to involve NTOs, TECs and RDAs as well as private and public enter-prises and education and training providers.

Initiated by the previous Government and continued by New Labour, a single network of NTOs is being formed to replace the more fragmented structure of ITOs, Lead Industry Bodies and Occupational Standards Councils. So far about 50 NTOs are in place and it was envisaged that a complete network of 110 would be in place by 1999 – a reduction from the 180 organizations in the previous network.

The formation of NTOs can be seen as a rationalization of complex and voluntarist employer-led structures rather than as a radical new policy departure. New Labour has, however, stressed the partnership role of NTOs and has given them some social as well as skill-based objectives (DfEE, 1997d). The rationale of the NTOs is to provide a more strategic mediating layer between government, TECs and employers and to address the neglect of skill needs at a sectoral level. Their educational remit reflects a more general trend towards the closer integration of education and training, including the development of NVQs and MAs within each sector.

Nevertheless, NTOs are still voluntary and self-financing, so that their strength and ability to encourage employers to invest more in training and development is variable. It remains to be seen how they will discharge their remit and how they will link with educational bodies at national and local level, though they are currently collaborating with the Qualifications and Curriculum Authority (QCA) over the development of NVQs. Their forma-tion, however, essentially continues the British voluntarist tradition, but aims to develop a more strategic voluntarist partnership rather than encour-aging a market-led model.

Below the sector-based and strategically-oriented NTOs lie geographi-cally-based TECs. Established in 1990/91, TECs were conceived as new locally-based and employer-led mechanisms within a market-led training system (Vickerstaff, 1998). Their strength is seen to lie in their potential to mobilize the local business community, though their main role still appears to be the implementation of government targets and programmes for the unemployed. Because of their market-oriented approaches, TECs have also developed in a variable way, reflecting both their locality and their own 'politics'. The overall effect of market-oriented short-termism has been that TECs have provided little push for the development of intermediate level skills (Vickerstaff, 1998; TUC, 1998). TECs will be needed by New Labour in the future and they, together with Chambers of Commerce, are currently being reviewed (DfEE, 1998n). One potential line of development is the encouragement of mergers between TECs and chambers of commerce to form Chambers of Commerce, Training and Enterprise (CCTEs). Sixteen mergers have already been approved and more are in the pipeline. Concern has been expressed, however, that these mergers could see a confusion of role for the newly-formed organizations 'requiring a Chinese Wall between the lobbying functions of the chamber, which must be funded through private money, and publicly-funded functions' (TUC, 1998: 7). Instead, reformers want to see an establishment of social partnership roles for TECs in collaboration with other major local players, including local authorities, education institutions, the careers service and unions (TUC, 1998).

RDAs, which will be established in 1999 and based on government office regions, could provide a new framework which looks beyond employers' current demands for skills and develops a more long-term provision of high quality VET (Rees, 1997). Furthermore, RDAs could promote collaborative projects (TUC, 1998). This will require partnerships, under the umbrella of RDAs, of local authorities, TECs and CCTEs, funding bodies such as the FEFC regions, educational institutions and unions.

Therefore, RDAs are required to respond to the context in which companies have previously adopted a low skills approach and, therefore, have tended to confront new skills shortages by either 'muddling through' or by poaching skilled workers (Green and Francis, 1992). These actions may make short-term sense to the company, though in the long run they run the risk of loss of competitiveness, but they do not result in a net improvement of skills available within an economy. It has been argued, therefore, that mechanisms have to be developed to address skills deficiencies rather than just specific skills shortages.[2] Such mechanisms could exist on both a sectoral basis (NTOs) and on a geographical regional basis (RDAs).

It is not yet clear whether New Labour intends to create a strong enough framework at a regional level to provide a more long-term supply of skills. The regional agenda constitutes a potentially radical theme in British politics and could form the basis for developing a strong social partnership approach. So far, however, the regional education and training agenda remains relatively unelaborated and subordinate to the current policy agendas of flexible labour markets and entrepreneurship highlighted in recent DfEE documents (for example DfEE, 1998n).

National Skills Taskforce

The National Skills Taskforce (NST) was set up by Rt Hon David Blunkett to advise on skills shortages and skills gaps in the UK and on how they might be addressed (DfEE, 1998k). Skills shortages have been defined by the NST as a shortage in the type of skill being sought which leads to difficulty in recruitment. The first report of the NST concludes that there are few shortages with the exception of IT specialists. The report goes on to recommend measures to help employers recruit more effectively and to use people coming off the New Deal. The term skills gaps, on the other hand, refers to a deficiency in the skills of existing employees or recruits which reduces business performance. In respect of skills gaps the report suggests that much of Government's response involves 'getting the general structure of the education and training system right' (DfEE, 1998k: 7).

It is also recommended that there should be further changes to the skills supply-side, including close co-operation between employer organizations, trade unions, NTOs, TECs and education and training providers to encourage employers to help staff upgrade their skills. New Labour sees the encouragement of skill development emerging from forms of partnership rather than from direct intervention by government. In this respect, the NST Report envisages an important role for the emerging RDAs in developing regional skills strategies. More specifically, the report recommends improving the information base about skills deficiencies; creating more connections between work-based learning and the education and training system; developing the 'softer Key Skills', such as problem-solving and working with others, in post-16 learning and training programmes; and the development of modular courses and more flexible qualifications. The NST could, therefore, be seen to be outlining a clearer social partnership approach to skills linked to reformed supply-side structures rather than simply depending on learner demand-led initiatives. One analyst observed that the Government-sponsored National Skills Task Force set to look at the 'skills gap' and 'skills shortages' managed to praise IiP, while mentioning UfI only once and not mentioning ILAs at all (Robinson, 1998a).

National Learning Targets for Young People and Adults

Another element of the Government's inheritance from the Conservatives was a set of national targets which aimed to promote international competitiveness. However, as the decade draws to an end, there has been increasing evidence that these national targets, which were revised in 1995, could not be met. Following a process of consultation, the Government set about renaming and revising the targets. First, it has created a more comprehensive set of targets in order to respond to both the social inclusion and the competitiveness agendas (Blackstone, 1998).[3] Second, the Government set what it thought were more achievable targets than those it inherited (eg 50 per cent of 16-year-olds to gain five GCSEs A–C by 2002, which will require only a four per cent rise in four years). Finally, a new 'Learning Participation Target' will soon be announced.

New Labour's approach to targets differs in two major respects from that of the Conservatives. First, they are broader and more achievable and thus more related to New Labour's own political goals rather than to the international comparative agenda. Second, they appear to focus more on the individual learner rather than the education and training system as a whole. However, the way in which they are similar to the national targets of the previous Government is that they are an exhortation to joint action in what is still a voluntaristic system.

NVQs and work-based qualifications

New Labour entered government with an ambivalent attitude to NVQs. Prior to the general election, New Labour saw the importance of NVQs in providing recognition of employees' skills and ensuring that employers' training requirements were given greater priority in the design and delivery of occupational qualifications (Labour Party, 1996b). At the same time, however, it recognized that NVQs had been subject to repeated criticism for being complex and jargon-ridden, narrow in the specification of knowledge and understanding and costly and bureaucratic to administer. New Labour stated that it would implement the recommendations of the Beaumont Report (Beaumont, 1995) which had suggested measures to strengthen vocational qualifications, including the development of more consistent forms of assessment. New Labour also suggested that NVQs required a further investigation beyond that carried out by the Beaumont Review.

Since 1997, New Labour has taken forward the Beaumont reform agenda which has, among other things, attempted to promote the role of knowledge in competence-based qualifications. At the same time, however, the new Government has also taken a more pragmatic, even positive, view of the role of traditional vocational qualifications, such as BTEC awards, which have persisted due to market demand for broader and more knowledge-based vocational qualifications. Rather than seeing them replaced by NVQs, which was the aim of the previous Government, New Labour has agreed that they should be brought into the national qualifications framework. However, while reviewing the role of NVQs, the Government has not undertaken the more fundamental review of their role indicated in *Aiming Higher* (Labour Party, 1996b). Instead, in conjunction with NTOs and QCA, it is seeking to adjust them pragmatically on a sector-by-sector basis (DfEE, 1997c).

From voluntarist initiatives to frameworks for social partnership

In this final part of the chapter, we will draw together the various strands of New Labour's current analysis and strategies for training and skills development in order to assess its likely progress in this area. The Government inherited a voluntarist and market-driven VET system which it decided to reform, not by a return to corporatist regulation, but by initiatives and partnerships aimed at promoting social inclusion and skills development. In this final section, we want to explore the implications of this approach to reform in terms of three strategic issues – different perspectives on competitiveness; the ability of the Government's current frameworks to bring about improvement; and the developing direction of the VET system.

Three versions of the competitiveness agenda

The Labour Government appears to be pursuing three competitiveness agendas related to low, intermediate and high level skills. We will argue that these three agendas are not yet strategically connected and each also raises different reform issues.

The first, in order of political priority, is what can be termed the 'voluntarist and social inclusion' competitiveness agenda. The focus here is on raising levels of numeracy and literacy among young people and basic skills among adults, tackling long-term unemployment and promoting employability. In compulsory education and in employment programmes, the Government is prepared to use high degrees of prescription in relation to the teaching profession, and compulsion, in relation to the unemployed, to bring the population up to a required minimum of literacy and skill. However, beyond these groups, voluntary mechanisms (eg UfI and ILAs) are being used to stimulate individual demand for training. There are considerable political virtues in this approach – they are high profile, they can produce measurable results to meet manifesto commitments and they may make in-roads into the problem of low achievement. However, beyond this these measures do not reform the way in which the whole education and training system functions and they may be becoming an excuse for not doing anything at this whole-system level. The key problem with this approach is that the very system problems it seeks to avoid may eventually undermine the capacity of the initiatives themselves to succeed.

Another approach to competitiveness could be termed the 'intermediate level skills and regulatory' agenda which has focused on the effects of the deficit of intermediate or Level 3 skills on the performance of UK industry. The intermediate skills arguments, which as we have seen, focus on whole-system problems, have resulted in three sets of proposals; first, for a degree of compulsion in relation to employer investment in skills and regulation of the youth labour market (Keep and Mayhew, 1997); second, building a strong alternance-based apprenticeship system with progression routes to higher education (Steedman et al, 1998); and third, stressing the importance of achievement of qualifications at Level 3 and beyond with implications, therefore, for the reform of A levels (Hodgson and Spours, 1997a).

Advocates of the 'intermediate levels skills and regulatory agenda' have tended, however, to neglect the issue of the provision for lower achievers, in part as a negative reaction to the poor quality and reputation of unemployment training schemes in the 1980s. Their approach has attracted criticism, on the grounds both of its lack of relevance to immediate labour market needs and on its elitism. Robinson (1998b) argues that there is little labour market justification for the attainment emphasis on Levels 3 and 4. The sectors which have traditionally provided apprenticeships are in relative decline and the Government could get far better returns for its investment by concentrating on the bottom 10 to 20 per cent of the population and getting them into employment.

A third perspective on competitiveness is associated with the Department of Trade and Industry (DTI)'s emphasis on the 'knowledge-based economy' and on developing the management of innovation (DTI, 1998). This emphasis on the management of innovation places the focus on development above Level 4 and raises issues about the role of higher education in relation to companies and competitiveness. It focuses on the high value-added and high-tech end of the competitiveness agenda. This perspective has visions of areas such as Cambridge providing the point of integration between leading-edge companies and university research; it focuses on the issue of regional and sub-regional co-ordination in relation to infrastructure and the supply of skills for both the leading companies and the companies which supply them. Like the intermediate level skills competitiveness arguments, the 'knowledge revolution' position has also attracted criticism on the grounds that it will end up producing a stratified hierarchy of the future labour market (Hatcher, 1998).

It is clear that all three competitiveness agendas are important, but currently they are not being viewed in relation to one another. The basic skills agenda is largely initiative-led, individualist and voluntarist, but with some draconian areas of compulsion; the intermediate skills agenda requires extensive system reform which the Government currently appears reluctant to contemplate; and the high skills agenda demands a geographically integrated approach which might be provided by robustly developed RDAs, but is currently undeveloped.

We argue that these skills levels and their reform agendas need to be connected in two different ways. First, there should be a concept of policy sequence and the creation of a new all-through competitiveness agenda – the current emphasis on basic skills will have to shift to a focus on intermediate skills so that people accessing basic skills provision do not remain locked into low-level courses and low-skilled jobs. A priority will be providing ladders of progression within VET provision. Second, the current emphasis on initiative-led voluntarist and partnership approaches will, at the point at which they fail to modify company behaviour, have to confront a more strategic planned agenda which will require radical reform in some areas. This theme is pursued further in the final chapter of this book through an exploration of the concept of 'weak' and 'strong' frameworks in New Labour's policies.

Notes

1   A 'mixed system' can be defined as one in which there is not a dominant mode of participation. In the mid/late 1980s, low levels of full-time participation were combined with significant entry into work-based training schemes and relatively large numbers of 16-year-olds moving into the youth labour market. This situation can be contrasted to France with its largely school-based education and training system and to that of Germany and Austria, with largely apprenticeship-based systems (Raffe, 1992). By the mid-1990s, the mixed system of the late 1980s had evolved into a school-based model due to the impact of rising levels of full-time participation. However, these plateaued at 70 per cent of 16-year-olds, 60 per cent of 17-year-olds and 40 per cent of 18-year-olds, compared to 80 per cent plus in competitor systems. The English/Welsh/NI system could, therefore, be described as a 'weak' school-based system.

2   A 'skills deficiency' can be defined as a shortfall in the broad structure of competencies required by a technologically advanced and value-added economy. The term 'skills shortage', on the other hand, is applied to the type of skills which, at any one moment, are not being adequately supplied by the labour market (DfEE, 1998k).

3   The new National Learning Targets for the year 2002 include 80 per cent of 11-year-olds reaching national standards in numeracy and literacy; 50 per cent of 16-year-olds getting five higher GCSEs and 95 per cent getting at least one GCSE; 85 per cent of 19-year-olds with a Level 2 qualification and 60 per cent of 21-year-olds with a Level 3 qualification; 50 per cent of adults with a Level 3 qualification and 28 per cent with a Level 4 qualification; 45 per cent of large/medium-sized organizations and 10,000 small organizations recognized as IiP (NACETT, 1998).

5

The Reform of Further and Higher Education

Introduction

Both further and higher education have been transformed over the past 10 years; yet there is widespread consensus that further reform is required in both sectors (Kennedy, 1997; NCIHE, 1997). This transformation has largely resulted from an unmanaged massification of the higher education system and a more planned but marketized expansion of the further education system, rather than from a strategic national approach to lifelong learning which spans both sectors.

Another factor which has shaped the role that further and higher education have played in the UK during the last 10 years is the lack of a strong work-based route in this country (Richardson *et al*, 1995). Viewed in this way, the role which further and higher education have played could be seen as a substitute for intervention in the labour market and the development of a stronger work-based education and training system in this country, in comparison with many other European and Scandinavian countries. In these latter countries, because of their tradition of strong social partnership, some of the education and training which is undertaken in further and higher education institutions in this country is seen as the responsibility of employers and is carried out in the workplace (OECD, 1998).

By the mid-1990s, and against the background of National Targets for Education and Training and the demands of the Competitiveness White Papers (DTI, 1994, 1995), the Conservative Government instituted a series of reviews of post-16 qualifications (Beaumont, 1995; Capey, 1996; Dearing, 1996), of further education (Kennedy, 1997) and of higher education (NCIHE, 1997). Taken together, these reviews were a recognition that the education and training system which had been shaped by the 1988 Education Reform Act (DES, 1988) and the 1992 Further and Higher Education Act (DfE, 1992) required further reform. Pressures for change were both internal and external. Internally, there were concerns about poor completion rates in further education and anxieties about maintaining standards in higher education. Externally, both sectors were expected to respond to wider economic and social pressures and to upskill and educate the population to meet the challenges of the new millennium. This was the institutional and sectoral context for the growing policy emphasis on lifelong learning and widening participation which, while predating New Labour, has been elevated by the new Government into a central 'policy discourse' for post-compulsory education. Both political parties, in recent national education policy documents (DfEE, 1996; DfEE, 1998a), have stressed the need for further and higher education, separately and in tandem, to change the way they operate in order to play a major role in supporting lifelong learning. This is reflected in the fact that the Kennedy review of further education (Kennedy, 1997) and the Dearing higher education review (NCIHE, 1997), although not strategically connected, both focus on the common themes of lifelong learning and widening participation.

New Labour's approach to the respective roles of further and higher education thus appears on the surface to be simple and compelling. Its central aim is to widen participation in education and training in order to address the problem of social exclusion and, thereby, to raise the skills levels of the population as a whole (Labour Party, 1996a; DfEE, 1998a).

While the Government recognizes the role that higher education has to play in society, its current emphasis has been on the expansion of further education as a way of tackling social and educational exclusion. In this respect, the most urgent task is how to recruit the target 700,000 students from the most excluded sections of society. New Labour is, therefore, putting in place a raft of initiatives in which further education will play a key role. These range from New Start to engage the 14–17-year-old 'disappeared', educational maintenance allowances to encourage post-16 participation of 'hard to get' sections of the age group and the New Deal aimed at unemployed 18–24-year-olds (see Chapters 3 and 4). Central to the short-term success of these initiatives is 'joined up thinking' and cross-agency collaboration linking further education, housing and welfare. In this area, as Chapter 3 points out, there is emerging evidence that the Government is working in an open-minded and imaginative way by looking to local pilot schemes that work best on the ground.

There is less evidence, however, that New Labour is ready to address the strategic roles of the further and higher education sectors and how they will relate to each other and to the education and training system as a whole. This is important, because an institutional framework needs to be put in place which not only provides for the excluded, but also creates a framework of progression for all groups. Tackling the legacy of the 'lost generation' is a vital first step, but it is only one dimension of future educational success which will depend on improved performance of all sections of the cohort.

While recognizing that it is important to view both sectors together when analysing New Labour's approach to reform in further and higher education, in this chapter we also discuss each sector separately. In this way, we are able to examine what the major implications of current policies are for each sector, as well as attempting to assess where policies designed for one sector might give rise to tensions within the other sector, and where they might contribute to the development of a more coherent education and training system for the 21st century. For each sector we cover the same three major themes – the case for reform, New Labour's approach to the sector and its policy proposals since coming to power in 1997 and, finally, key issues arising from this approach. The chapter concludes with a section which speculates what the implications of New Labour's approach to the reform of further and higher education might be for the future of the post-compulsory sector as a whole and indicates challenges which still remain to be addressed in this Parliament and beyond.

The case for reform of further education

There has been an unprecedented expansion and diversification of further education provision over the last five years, largely as a result of the incorporation of further education colleges and specific funding steers from the Further Education Funding Council (FEFC). The sector currently caters for over 4 million students, 80 per cent of whom are adults, taking some 17,000 different qualifications (DfEE, 1998o). On one level, this can be seen as a considerable success for further education. At the same time, however, unit costs have fallen by 12 per cent (DfEE, 1998a) and several further education colleges are reported to be in financial difficulty (Education and Employment Committee, 1998). Moreover, there is widespread concern about the quality of some of the provision being offered by further education colleges (particularly where this has been franchised out) and suspicion that employers are using public further education funding to subsidize training they should be providing themselves (Education and Employment Committee, 1998). The sector is also suffering from low staff morale as a result of protracted battles over contracts and the significant changes brought about by the twin processes of incorporation and experimentation with a new national funding methodology (Green and Lucas, 1999).

However, the further education sector, as many of the government's recent policy documents testify, is viewed as central to New Labour's lifelong learning project. There is thus considerable consensus both within and outside further education colleges that the sector will need reform and support if it is to fulfil this mission (Education and Employment Committee, 1998). The challenges for New Labour could be seen as threefold: to rescue the sector from its current financial difficulties; to clarify the regional and national roles which further education is expected to play in promoting and supporting lifelong learning now and in the future; and to provide the infrastructure within which the sector can carry out this role.

New Labour's approach to the further education sector

Two of New Labour pre-election documents discuss the role of further education in the education and training system as a whole – *Learn as You Earn: Labour's plans for a skills revolution* (Labour Party, 1996c) and, to a much lesser degree, *Lifelong Learning* (Labour Party, 1996d). We suggest that the themes which are laid out in these two documents have broadly set the agenda that New Labour has pursued in further education since coming to power in May 1997, although the influence of the Kennedy Report, *Learning Works* (Kennedy, 1997), which was commissioned under the Conservative administration but was published shortly after New Labour took office, has also been considerable and has possibly changed the emphasis of some of New Labour's policies in this area.

Here we describe the four central themes set out in *Lifelong Learning* and *Labour's Plans for a Skills Revolution* (funding further education, the role of local partnerships and regional planning, increasing local accountability and improving quality) and examine to what extent and in what ways these themes have been translated into policy under New Labour. We then turn to two newer themes – widening participation and the basic skills agenda – which we argue were not strongly in evidence prior to the election, but have now become of crucial importance to New Labour's approach to the reform of further education, as well as to the principles underlying its Comprehensive Spending Review. Finally, we end this section of the chapter by suggesting that the question of a national role or identity for the further education sector has not yet been adequately addressed, despite the importance and urgency of this task.

Funding further education

In *Lifelong Learning* (Labour Party, 1996a), New Labour has three major proposals in relation to the funding of further education provision. First, it suggests that there is a need for more money for the sector. Second, it proposes there should be a review of the FEFC's funding methodology in order to ensure quality and standards, to provide better support for disadvantaged learners and to meet specific local needs. Third, there is an undertaking to look into a more equitable way of funding post-16 provision across schools, colleges and training providers. Additionally, the document put forward two measures in relation to financial support for individual learners in further education colleges. There is a promise to make changes to the 16-hour rule, which prevents many students from studying while claiming benefit, and to review the discretionary awards system.

Since coming to power, New Labour has begun to follow up all these undertakings and has made providing more money for the further education sector one of its priorities in relation to post-compulsory education and training policy. It has published two policy papers – *The Learning Age*

(DfEE, 1998a) and *Further Education for the New Millennium* (DfEE, 1998o) – which have put forward proposals for additional funding for further education that have then been supported by decisions in the Comprehensive Spending Review (DfEE, 1998p). In addition, two major national advisory groups – the Education and Employment Committee on Further Education and the Fryer Committee – have been asked to examine further education funding issues as a major part of their brief. Finally, there has been an advisory group set up under the chairmanship of Graham Lane to make recommendations about effective student support in further education (DfEE, 1998q), while the FEFC has been set the task of reviewing the way it funds the sector and of responding to funding proposals in the Kennedy Report.

The Government still has to give its response to some of the detailed recommendations put forward by these different advisory groups, but there appear to be a number of key themes emerging. The first is that New Labour is unlikely to make radical changes to the FEFC's funding model or to the process of convergence towards a more common unit tariff across the sector, although there is a desire for simplification. The second is that there will be more money for further education, but that this is contingent on an improvement in quality and student retention and to be targeted at certain national priorities, such as widening participation (DfEE, 1998p). A third emerging approach is that there will be more commonality between the way different post-16 providers are funded. Finally, there will be changes to the way that discretionary awards are handled so that there is better financial support for 16–19-year-old learners in further education (DfEE, 1998p). What is not yet clear is exactly what minor changes will be made to the FEFC funding model to make it easier to understand and apply; when common funding systems for all post-16 providers will be brought in; whether individual financial support will apply to part-time as well as to full-time learners; and how this support for individuals will be financed (eg through changes to child benefits or other mechanisms).

Until some of these issues have been resolved, it is not possible to pass a balanced judgement on the extent of New Labour's commitment to funding a high quality and equitable further education sector. What is clear, however, is that this administration has taken the sector's financial position seriously and is putting into place policies designed to strengthen its position as a major player in the Government's lifelong learning project.

The role of local partnerships and regional planning in further education

There are three New Labour pre-election policy documents which consider the role of local partnerships and regional planning in relation to further education – *Lifelong Learning* (Labour Party, 1996a), *Labour's Plans for a Skills Revolution* (Labour Party, 1996g) and, in passing, *Aiming Higher*

(Labour Party, 1996b). In all three documents there is strong criticism of the Conservative Government's market approach to education and training, which is seen as wasteful and divisive, as well as damaging in terms of student choice. The policy response is collaboration through local partnerships and regional planning with the ultimate goal of achieving a 'regional framework for tertiary education' (Labour Party, 1996a: 11) to meet national government priorities for post-16 education and training. The *Lifelong Learning* document emphasizes a strategic role for the FEFC's regional committees, the Government's regional offices and the newly proposed RDAs. *Labour's Plans for a Skills Revolution* stresses the need for closer collaboration between further education providers and employers, possibly via initiatives such as ILAs and IiP and *Aiming Higher* underlines the importance of strong local partnerships between TECs, LEAs and further education colleges.

Support for local partnerships and regional planning has continued to be a feature of New Labour's policy documents in the area of post-compulsory education and training since the election. *The Learning Age*, for example, supports the idea of a 'regional framework for tertiary education' (DfEE, 1998a: 47), suggests that there should be strategic planning taking place at a local and regional level led by RDAs and announces a Collaboration Fund to support such work. *Further Education for the New Millennium* (DfEE, 1998o) includes a whole chapter on partnerships and indicates the type of local and regional partnerships which will be set up to support initiatives such as the Investing in Young People Strategy,[1] the UfI,[2] employee development schemes, IiP and the New Deal.[3] The key players at the regional level are seen to be the RDAs, the FEFC Regional Committees, LEAs, further education colleges, higher education institutions and TECs, although there is little information yet on exactly how collaborative partnerships between these different players are to be achieved, whether they will have resources (and if so how much) and who will be considered as the lead partner or partners.

As Baroness Blackstone, Minister for Education, indicated at a press launch for the consultation document *Accountability in Further Education* (DfEE, 1998r), local partnerships are seen by this administration not only as cost-effective, but also as a mechanism for raising standards in post-16 education and training: 'In recent years too many institutions have been distracted from their real task by the demands of a competitive market in post-16 education. This has led to expensive duplication of provision and has undermined the effective local partnerships that can support high standards' (DfEE, 1998s).

What this partnership and collaborative approach to post-16 education and training does not address explicitly is the potential need to rationalize provision or even to reorganize institutional structures in certain areas. There has been considerable criticism recently, for example, of the costs of small sixth forms (Rafferty, 1998), but there does not appear to be any indication in any of New Labour's policy documents or ministerial announcements that it intends to confront this problem head on by developing tertiary systems in local areas. There may well, therefore, be some tough decisions to be made by any new local and regional partnerships which are formed. It will remain to be seen how this type of collaboration develops; how the new partnerships relate to the work of the National Skills Task Force, in terms of skills development and strategic planning at the local and regional level; and whether partnerships manage to tackle the worst excesses of the market in education and training.

Accountability

A third and related area where New Labour has been proactive since coming into power has been the area of accountability in further education. This can be seen partly as a desire to raise standards in public education institutions, and in further education in particular because of concerns about low quality and mismanagement, but also (and perhaps more importantly) the wish to ensure more democratic accountability to stakeholders and the community as a whole.

In the summer of 1998, the Government published a consultation paper, *Accountability in Further Education* (DfEE, 1998r), which suggested the need for the reform of further education colleges' governing bodies to make them broader based. Because of the key role further education is intended to play locally and regionally, it is suggested in this document that there should be greater representation by TECs, local authorities, college staff, students and others representing community interests. There is also an emphasis on accounts and college plans being more open to public scrutiny, with an annual open meeting as well as the preparation of an annual public report.

Quality

The issue of raising standards in further education provision is one which was in strong evidence in New Labour's pre-election policy documents and which has been continued in government. *The Learning Age* (DfEE, 1998a) talks about harmonizing inspection systems across the whole post-16 education and training system and about developing a national framework for inspection with common procedures and grading. There is a desire to make further education colleges accountable in a similar way to schools by giving them annual targets to improve retention and achievement. They will also be asked to measure 'value-added' or 'learning gain' and will be expected to publish their results annually alongside schools.

The other major way in which New Labour seeks to improve the quality of further education is by requiring all full-time and substantial part-time teachers in further education colleges to hold or, within two years of appointment, to have begun a recognized initial teacher training qualification. Since the publication of its Green Paper, the Government has established a sector-specific organization, the Further Education National Training Organization (FENTO), to realize this policy initiative and to develop a national framework for management development in further education.

The importance which New Labour attaches to this area of policy has been demonstrated recently at the Association of Colleges 1998 Annual Conference, when David Blunkett announced new money for the further education sector, but indicated that it was dependent upon further education providers raising the quality of provision and delivery (Crequer, 1998).

Widening participation and securing basic skills

There are two major themes which did not figure strongly in New Labour's pre-election policy documents on further education, but which now appear central to the Government's approach to the sector – widening participation and securing basic skills. These themes are clearly interrelated and also play an important part in the social inclusion and lifelong learning agendas. Their importance is continually stressed in *The Learning Age* (DfEE, 1998a) and two of the key policy initiatives which are contained in this document – ILAs and UfI – are seen as playing a strong role in addressing both widening participation and securing basic skills for all. Moreover, many of the funding levers outlined in this document are designed to encourage institutions to focus on widening participation and to provide incentives for learners to improve their basic skills. Similarly, a major part of *Further Education for the New Millennium* (DfEE, 1998o) is devoted to these two issues and includes a clear undertaking by the Government that it intends to see them as a priority for funding. New Labour has also set up a special committee, under the chairmanship of Sir Claus Moser, to investigate the problem of basic skills and to suggest ways of tackling it. Meanwhile, the FEFC has published its own guidance on how further education colleges might go about widening participation (FEFC, 1997) and has developed ways of incentivizing providers to increase access, achievement and progression for those learners who have traditionally been under-represented in further education provision.

In terms of developments in the further education sector, it is clear that the issues of widening participation and securing basic skills are to some extent dominating the agenda. One can only speculate on why these issues might have emerged as so important to New Labour early on in government, when they were not perceived to be so significant prior to election. One reason is undoubtedly that the Kennedy Report (1997), whose central concern was to widen participation in learning, had an impact on New Labour, coming as it did so early on in the new administration and being so closely related to the Government's increasing focus on the emerging social exclusion problem.

However, it is interesting that the one aspect of the Kennedy Report which the Government has not addressed is its focus on an entitlement to free provision up to NVQ Level 3 (A level/Advanced Level GNVQ/NVQ Level 3 or equivalent) for those who have not achieved this level in compulsory schooling. The Government's response to this request, which is outlined in *Further Education for the New Millennium*, is somewhat non-committal, with a definite stress on the importance of Level 2 rather than Level 3 entitlement. This might be seen as a purely financial response to what may have turned out to be a very costly entitlement, but it might also suggest that New Labour's agenda was already being determined by its concern with the large number of UK adults without basic skills and the need to address this problem.

It could be argued that New Labour's strong initial focus on the important issues of widening participation and securing basic skills has had an important effect on debates about the strategic role for further education now and in the future. First, we would suggest that these issues have tended to take precedence over debates about the wider purposes of the sector and the interface between further and higher education. Second, it appears that discussion of how further education might contribute to the development of higher level skills, particularly vocational skills, which many believe are vital to the competitiveness agenda in this country (Finegold and Soskise, 1988; Steedman and Green, 1997; Keep and Mayhew, 1997) has taken a rather poor second place.

Key issues arising from New Labour's approach to further education

We believe there are four issues which arise from New Labour's overall approach to further education to date. First, as we have indicated above, there is a concern that policy in this area has been over-influenced by the widening participation and basic skills agenda. No one could deny the importance of this focus, but the way that it has been used by this Government tends to place too strong a reliance on supply-side measures, such as access to the education system, to redress the widening economic, social and cultural differences between people in this country. If one looks at the following quotation from *The Learning Age*, for example: 'It (the Government) sees further education as the key to breaking the vicious circle of poor economic performance and an inadequate standard of living' (DfEE, 1998n: 47). One is tempted to agree with writers such as Coffield (1997), Macrae *et al* (1997) and others that simply inviting more people to participate in further education is not enough. There is also a need to examine more carefully some of the underpinning structural reasons for inequality, which lie beyond the education and training system itself. In particular, in relation to further education, it is important to consider developing a more active relationship between the labour market and the education and training system, such as that which exists in many other European countries through social partnership arrangements (Rees, 1997; Green, 1997).

Second, as indicated above, the focus on further education's role in widening participation and improving the basic skills of the population has tended to dominate debates about the sector. This has meant that the important debates about how further education relates to higher education, employers and the world of work in order to promote and support the development of a high skills economy have been less fully aired or explored. It is interesting, for example, that the first report from the National Skills Task Force (DfEE, 1998j) does not specifically mention either further education or the relationship between employers and further education in developing the national skills base. It is as if learning in the workplace is seen as something quite separate from the type of learning which takes place in further (or higher) education.

While this emphasis on basic skills and second chance learning makes sense in relation to the priority of educational and social inclusion, it begs the question of further education's strategic national or regional role in relation to the different dimensions of competitiveness raised in Chapter 4. Currently, despite the existence of a single national funding body for further education, because of the considerable autonomy of individual colleges, further education cannot be seen as a genuinely national sector. The Education and Employment Committee on Further Education (1998) suggests that this would only become a reality if there were adequate funding for further education, a template for national conditions of service for further education staff and greater clarity about the sector's mission both nationally and regionally. Arguably, this role would also require a strong national framework of inspection and quality assurance, common post-16 funding and a common national qualifications system to underpin the concept of a tertiary system at local and regional level.

Paradoxically, the issue of a strategic national role or identity for further education is likely to be highlighted by the role it will increasingly be expected to play in local and regional collaboration. Successful collaboration is only possible where individual partners feel they are coming from a solid baseline. There is no doubt that strong local and regional planning and funding bodies could have a powerful part to play in creating the kind of productive and strategic partnerships between employers, trade unions and education and training providers, which New Labour sees as its longer-term response to the negative effects of marketization in education and training (Pearce and Hillman, 1998). However, at present there are too many bodies involved – RDAs, TECs, LEAs and FEFC Regional Committees – with no clear indication of their individual or complementary roles. Similarly, there is a plethora of different funding streams, each with its own bureaucratic requirements and many of which are subject to competitive bidding and likely, therefore, to create competition rather than collaboration between potential partners.

Funding-driven reform of further education has forced its diversification to the point at which colleges are becoming unclear about their role and mission. Widening participation could either be seen as an extension of the logic of taking all-comers or it could force a process of role clarification. Regional and local collaboration may tip the balance, where in relation to other partners, colleges will have to define what they are really about. In particular, they will have to address areas of overlap with other providers, the most evident of which are courses for 16–19-year-olds and their relationship with schools; vocational provision at Levels 2 and 3 and their relationship with employers; and progression into Level 4 and beyond and their relationship with higher education. It is to this last sector which we now turn.

Higher education – the case for reform

The two major recent national reforms which have had the greatest impact on higher education have been the Education Reform Act of 1988 and the Further and Higher Education Act of 1992. The first replaced the University Grants Committee with the University Funding Council, thus placing the relationship between the state and the universities on a statutory basis for the first time (Salter and Tapper, 1994). The second got rid of the binary divide between polytechnics and universities and introduced incorporation of colleges, thus stimulating a quasi-market in both higher and further education. It also set up the Higher Education Funding Councils in England, Northern Ireland, Wales and Scotland for all types of higher education institutions, thereby ensuring that the state had more control over the sector through the lever of funding mechanisms. These two reforms, together with wider socio-economic changes which took place during the late 1980s and early 1990s, resulted in such a radical change to the size, shape and financial position of higher education that, by the mid 1990s, the Conservative administration felt there was a need for a major review of the sector.

Thus, in 1996, the National Committee of Inquiry into Higher Education under the Chairmanship of Sir Ron Dearing was given the task of making recommendations on how: 'the purposes, shape, structure, size and funding of higher education, including support for students, should develop to meet the needs of the UK over the next 20 years, recognising that higher education embraces teaching, learning, scholarship and research' (NCIHE, 1997: 5).

Although the Committee was set up by the Rt Hon Gillian Shephard, Conservative Secretary of State at the time, it had bipartisan support for its work and, according to Scott (1997), the Minister was persuaded to include a number of New Labour supporters among its members. This indicates a strong national consensus on the importance of reforming higher education in the UK.

However, the view that higher education needs to change to meet the demands of the 21st century is not confined to the UK; both the OECD (OECD, 1996) and the European Union (SOCRATES Project, 1998) are commissioning international studies to examine the future role and purpose of higher education. International economic, political, demographic and social trends are forcing many countries to radically rethink the purpose and future direction of their higher education sectors.

Despite these international trends, the Dearing Committee was primarily a response to changed conditions in the UK system over the last decade. As suggested earlier in the chapter, higher education had changed dramatically from a divided and quasi-autonomous sector designed largely for young adults to a single, nationally directed and partially marketized system for learners of all ages. During this 10-year period, the number of full-time students had increased, part-time study had become commonplace, many more women were undertaking higher study and mature students were an absolute majority of all entrants to higher education (McNair, 1998). The idea of a common student experience of higher education is, therefore, effectively a thing of the past.

Changing patterns of participation have also been reflected in the curriculum which, in many higher education institutions, has been vocationalized, marketized and modularized (Williamson, 1996). There is now a single higher education sector with one funding body (rather than two), but the differences between institutions within the sector has increased rather than decreased. Research and teaching are increasingly seen as separate functions and there is a growing focus on applied rather than basic or strategic research (Salter and Tapper, 1994). Moreover, higher education institutions are more often having to compete with enterprises and private research consultancies for research contracts and are no longer seen as the sole producers of new knowledge (Gibbons, 1996).

Perhaps most importantly, certainly in the short term, public *per capita* funding for higher education students has fallen (NCIHE, 1997) and, since higher education institutions are more dependent on state funding that in any other part of Europe (Salter and Tapper, 1994), they are thus financially stretched. Within this changing context, the autonomy enjoyed by the traditional universities has been seriously eroded by the increased influence of central government officials, while local government has been squeezed out of the picture altogether since 1992.

A crisis of role and identity: the Dearing response

A period of rapid and relatively unmanaged growth, increased institutional differentiation within a more unified sector, the emergence of competition with other knowledge-producing agencies and a funding squeeze have all contributed to a sense of crisis in higher education. Academics and students complain about declining resources and conditions and employers are concerned about the lack of adequately skilled graduates; while the Government worries about standards on the one hand, and widening participation on the other.

As part of a 'managed market' in education (Salter and Tapper, 1994), higher education institutions are neither fully exposed to the vagaries and buffets of a free market, in which they would be forced to modernize to become part of a more open and flexible lifelong learning system, nor are they able to hold on to their traditionally independent position, because they are increasingly exposed to the vocal demands of the Government, learners and others who fund them. Higher education's strategic role thus remains unclear. Currently the sector appears to be caught between two stools – the need to retain its position as an elite internationally recognized sector with an independent view on the society in which it finds itself; and the demand for it to play a major role in the government's strategy for a flexible and responsive lifelong learning system for the future. Moreover, it has all the immediate pressing problems associated with the legacy of an unmanaged and underfunded massification of the sector.

Around the central question of what the role and purpose of higher education in the 21st century should be and how it should respond to the global challenges arising from that context, a number of key debates emerged during the consultation process surrounding the National Committee of Inquiry into Higher Education (NCIHE). These can be broadly divided into four interrelated areas:

1. the problem of how higher education institutions manage the balance between research and teaching and whether there is a need for specialist institutions with different missions;
2. how higher education should be funded and who should pay for it;
3. what the curriculum in higher education institutions should be, what part student choice should play in this and how the curriculum might be delivered, including through the use of ICT;
4. improving the quality of the teaching, learning and research taking place in higher education institutions.

Despite the fact that the NCIHE set out specifically to explore the central issue of the role and purpose of higher education in the 21st century and took account of the four key debates outlined above, there still appears to be a lack of clarity about what the core purpose and central direction of the sector should be. The Dearing Report, which has been unfavourably compared with the earlier Robbins Report (1963), has been criticized both for its limited scope and vision (Scott, 1997) and for its lack of a radical plan for change (McNair, 1998).

However, it is important that these criticisms are seen in the light of the very different national and international context within which higher education finds itself in the late 1990s. There is a growing focus now on the effects of globalization and world economic trends, the impact of information and communications technologies and the role of international companies as well as international higher education in competing for research and students.

Higher education has been thrust into the national and international education, training and research market in a way that would have been inconceivable in the 1960s at the time of the Robbins Report. These developments are
seen by many to pose significant challenges to establishing the future role and
direction of any national higher education system in the changing international social, economic and political context at the end of the 20th century
(Barnett, 1994; Scott, 1995; Coffield and Williamson, 1997).

Labour's approach to higher education

The task facing New Labour in 1997 was, therefore, twofold. First, to
address the immediate practical (and particularly financial) problems of the
sector resulting from the Conservative legacy and the wider national and
international socio-economic context. Second, to bring in reforms which
would help to shape higher education's strategic role for the future. We would
suggest that, at the time of writing this chapter, there is some evidence that
New Labour is tackling the former, but that the strategy behind policies to
address the latter is still unclear, despite the crucial importance of the task.

There appear to be two guiding principles behind New Labour's current
approach to higher education – building economic prosperity and promoting
social justice. In this very broad sense, there is little to distinguish New
Labour's approach from that of Old Labour. On the other hand, there are
some clear breaks from the past. The idea of two sectors of higher education
– the autonomous universities and the publicly owned 'separate but equal'
polytechnics (Crosland, 1965) for example – has entirely disappeared.
There is also little left of the idea of a locally planned but centrally directed
comprehensive 18+ education system (Labour Party, 1973), unless New
Labour's support for lifelong learning could be seen as a weak echo of this
earlier policy proposal.

During the 1980s and early 1990s there appeared to be little difference
between the policies of the two major political parties in relation to higher
education. In the early 1990s, Labour's two major documents on higher
education – *Quality Assured* (Labour Party, 1991) and *The Open University*
(Labour Party, 1992b) – were neither comprehensive in scope nor particularly challenging in terms of a critique of the Conservative Party's approach
to this area of policy.

In 1996, however, New Labour published its *Lifelong Learning* document
(Labour Party, 1996a) which had a substantial section on higher education.
This document attempted both to articulate New Labour's strategic
approach to this area and to translate New Labour's underlying principles of
'equality, access, equity and accountability' into concrete policy proposals.

Lifelong Learning stresses the need for a review of the role of higher education in the 21st century with a particular emphasis on the sector's contribution to employment and to active citizenship. There is also a focus on higher

education's local and regional, as well as its national and international roles. The other main areas which it covers and which are largely echoed in New Labour's response to the Dearing Report, *Higher Education for the 21st Century* (DfEE, 1998b), include support for widening and increasing participation in higher education (with an end to the cap on higher education expansion); greater choice and flexibility for students; support for a specific higher education agency to ensure standards and quality; professional accreditation of higher education teaching; the need to review funding for both teaching and research; a particular focus on the role of higher education in promoting science and technology; and the need to develop ICT.

These areas will be discussed in more detail below. However, it is perhaps first worth highlighting here two key areas where New Labour's *Lifelong Learning* document differs from its approach in government – the development of a national credit framework and the introduction of tuition fees for students. The first might be considered a difference of emphasis, though nonetheless important; the second can only be seen as a *volte face*. *Lifelong Learning* appears to be suggesting the development of a national credit framework which covers both further and higher education, whereas what New Labour ends up supporting in *Higher Education for the 21st Century* appears to be the much more limited concept of a higher education framework. In relation to tuition fees for students, there is a clear statement in *Lifelong Learning* which sets out New Labour's views on the subject: '*Labour opposes up-front tuition fees*' (Labour Party, 1996: 33). This position has, then, been reversed early in New Labour's term of government.

New Labour's response to Dearing

As we have noted earlier, New Labour was represented on the National Committee of Inquiry into Higher Education, despite the fact that this Committee was set up under a Conservative administration. Moreover, the Committee reported after New Labour had come into power. It is perhaps therefore hardly surprising that many of the recommendations in the Dearing Report echo much of New Labour's pre-election higher education policy and that in government New Labour felt able, in its response to the Dearing Report, *Higher Education for the 21st Century*, to support many of that report's recommendations. Since it is this response document which provides the most comprehensive published record of New Labour's approach to higher education and which also sets the agenda for many of its future policies in this area, we examine it in some detail here before raising some issues related to this approach.

Higher Education for the 21st Century consists of 11 chapters each of which starts with a brief statement on the Government's views on a particular area and then sets out and responds to relevant recommendations from the Dearing Report. All 93 recommendations from the Report are thus considered in a thematic way. We do not propose to discuss all of these here, rather we wish to single out one major overarching theme and five interrelated sub-themes for brief discussion, since these appear to us to be of particular importance to the New Labour project in this area and to provide a flavour of New Labour's approach. All six relate strongly to the twin underlying principles of building economic prosperity and promoting social justice mentioned earlier.

Modernizing higher education

The overarching theme of New Labour's approach to higher education, as to many other areas of policy within and beyond education, is the need to modernize. Modernization in relation to higher education means widening access to teaching and learning, particularly for young people from disadvantaged backgrounds, raising standards of research and teaching in order to compete in a global market, becoming more responsive to the needs of employers and the economy, exploiting new technologies and research, particularly in science, and sharing the costs of higher education with those who benefit from it.

To some extent this does not differ substantially from the previous government's agenda for higher education, although the emphasis in New Labour's approach is somewhat different. It is no accident, for example, that the first chapter in *Higher Education for the 21st Century* is entitled 'Increasing participation and widening access' and emphasizes both the importance of lifting the cap on student numbers and opening the doors to those who have not traditionally benefited from higher education. This is the social justice agenda and it comes both before the chapter on 'Quality and standards' and the one on 'Higher education's links to the economy and employability'.

Widening participation

New Labour's strategy for widening participation in higher education is four-fold – to use a variety of funding levers to support higher education institutions in widening participation; to provide targeted individual support for particular groups of under-represented learners (eg those with disabilities); to increase the number of sub-degree programmes designed to attract new types of learners; and to focus attention on the kind of teaching and learning strategies required for the new types of learners entering higher education. In order to monitor the effectiveness of this strategy, the government indicates that it will set specific targets for institutions to meet in terms of widening participation and that it will monitor the effects of its various policies in this area through the collection of relevant statistical data.

Moreover, since the publication of *Higher Education for the 21st Century*, the Higher Education Funding Council for England (HEFCE) has brought out a consultation document outlining the ways in which it proposes to encourage institutions to widen participation through specific funding steers (HEFCE, 1998).

There is no doubt that this strategy will put considerable pressure on higher education institutions to consider their position in relation to widening participation. However, it is likely that while some institutions will see widening participation as central to their mission, others may be tempted to ignore the funding 'carrots' on offer and to focus more narrowly on retaining their elite position. There is a danger that funding mechanisms of this type, while powerful, might lead to a polarization of higher education institutions and that learners from disadvantaged backgrounds may well be effectively denied a real choice of institution in which to study.

Learning and teaching

'Learning and teaching' is the title of the third chapter in *Higher Education for the 21st Century* and again it is important to note its position in the document. It comes before the chapter on research and is a plea to enhance the status of teaching in higher education in relation to research, as well as to improve the quality of teaching and learning that takes place. Perhaps it is also significant that the title of the chapter puts learning in front of teaching: this is very much in tune with the lifelong learning (rather than lifelong education) agenda.

It is in this chapter that the Government indicates its support for the new Institute for Learning and Teaching in Higher Education (ILTHE) which, among other tasks, will have overall responsibility for accrediting programmes of teacher training for higher education lecturers (although here, as later in the document, the Government stops short of requiring all lecturers to undertake accreditation of this sort). In this respect, there is an interesting difference between the demands which are being made for higher education and those which are being made for all other sectors (including further education) where accreditation is already, or will be, a requirement for employment.

A second major issue which is highlighted in this chapter, and which can be seen as linked to the idea of modernization outlined above, is the need for programmes to be more relevant to the needs of students and employers by promoting skills for employability.

A further area which relates to learning and teaching, but which is dealt with elsewhere in the report, is ICT. As in other New Labour documents on education and training, ICT is seen as central to the mission of widening access to and participation in learning. It is recommended, although again not required, that all higher education institutions should develop an ICT strategy and management expertise in this area. There is also a suggestion that funding might be made available, following the Comprehensive Spending Review, to ensure that all students have open access to a networked desk computer by 2000/2001.

The relationship between higher education and the outside world

Running throughout *Higher Education for the 21st Century* is the idea that higher education needs to be more responsive to its local and regional communities, as well as to its more traditional national and international markets and academic communities. One of New Labour's key policy initiatives in this area is the setting up of RDAs. It is envisaged that higher education institutions should play a key role within these agencies, in addition to the role they are expected to play within the older FEFC Regional Committees and within the TECs. This strategy might be seen as strengthening the regional voice or, more cynically, as a recipe for confusion. It is unclear as yet what the relationship between all three of these agencies will be and to what extent any or all of them will be able to use funding incentives to support higher education institutions in developing their regional role. What is clear, however, is that New Labour wishes to tie higher education in more closely with its local and regional communities as part of its 'contribution to competitiveness and prosperity' (DfEE, 1998a: 34).

Research in higher education

From the 1960s, when universities, and later polytechnics, were seen as key players in the post-war 'technological and scientific revolution', the need to support high quality research, particularly in the areas of science and technology, has been a constant theme in Labour policy documents on higher education. New Labour continues this theme by recognizing some of the weaknesses in the way in which research is currently funded and supporting many of the recommendations for reform laid out in the Dearing Report. There is a particular focus on the research links between industry and higher education institutions, explicit encouragement for joint public–private sector research initiatives and more public and private funding is being channelled into science research via the Department of Trade and Industry as well as the Research Councils.

What is not yet clear is the Government's view on whether research should be largely concentrated in a smaller number of higher education institutions, in order to create centres of excellence which are able to maintain a competitive edge in international markets, or whether there will be a desire for all higher education institutions to develop their own individual research capacity. This is an issue which is likely to prove controversial in higher education circles.

Funding higher education

As indicated earlier in this chapter, one of the most immediate problems facing New Labour when it came into power in May 1997 was the crisis of funding in both higher and further education. Both sectors had seen 10 years of unprecedented expansion, accompanied by diminishing units of funding in real terms.

Very early in its administration, New Labour committed itself to addressing this situation by spending a higher proportion of national income on higher and further education, as well as on compulsory education. However, there is no indication that it is likely to take a new or radical approach to the way in which higher education is funded overall by, for example, overturning the previous administration's introduction of a single funding council for the sector. Policies to date, such as those around widening participation (HEFCE, 1998), suggest that New Labour, like the previous administration, will continue to use targeted funding mechanisms as the major tool for shaping and influencing the future direction of higher education.

Despite the lack of radical overall change in this area, one of New Labour's approaches to increasing the amount of money available for higher education – that is, the introduction of fees for all undergraduate courses – has proved to be one of its most controversial policies to date. New Labour's decision to introduce student fees was all the more surprising because it had not been trailed in any of its pre-election documents, although it was proposed by the National Committee of Inquiry into Higher Education.

Unfortunately for New Labour, this policy has not only dominated the debates about higher education and obscured many of the other initiatives which are being proposed in this area, but has also been criticized from within the Labour Party, as well as by members of both Opposition Parties. In many cases, the policy has been poorly understood and the in-built safety mechanisms for students from disadvantaged backgrounds have been either under-publicized or ignored by those who argue for 'free higher education'. The fact that education has not been free for many postgraduate students and the vast majority of part-time adult learners often gets overlooked; so too, do the statistics which demonstrate that previous policies on undergraduate fees have not managed to reduce the higher education participation gap between those from higher and lower socio-economic groups (Coffield and Vignoles, 1997; Robertson and Hillman, 1997).

The introduction of a £1,000 annual tuition fee for all undergraduates, which represents about a quarter of the average cost of a higher education programme, is seen primarily as a way of reinforcing New Labour's underlying idea that individuals need to take more responsibility for their own learning and that those who benefit from education should also contribute financially towards it. This same theme runs through their approach to maintenance grants which will, in most cases, be replaced by loans, repayable through income tax when the graduate's annual earnings have reached £10,000 (DfEE, 1998a).

The problem for New Labour is that there has been a reduction in the number of people applying for higher education, with a disproportionate drop in those over 25. According to University and College Admissions Service figures (UCAS, 1999), the number of applicants for entry to higher education in autumn 1999 is down by 1.8 per cent on 1998 (which itself had lower figures than the previous year) and for those who are 25 or over, this year's figure represents a fall of 18.3 per cent. The Government's response has been to make a loan of £500 available for course expenses for the first time for low-income part-time students in higher education (THES, 1999). However, there are concerns that this will not be enough to attract back into higher education the group of adult learners which New Labour has continually stressed it wishes to attract into lifelong learning.

The idea of increasing private as well as public investment in lifelong learning, and particularly higher education (since there is stronger evidence of good individual rates of return to participation in higher education than to participation in other types of education and training) is not unique to this government and is one which many other countries are currently considering (OECD, 1998). However, in New Labour's approach to this area, there is also a strong commitment to equity through the use of safeguards for students from lower income families. There is, in addition, possibly the beginning of a desire to move towards more funding following the student, in order to make higher education institutions more responsive to student demands. This latter approach, which was hinted at in pre-election policy documents (Labour Party, 1996a), and which has been strongly supported by academics such as Robertson (1996c), only makes the odd appearance in *Higher Education in the 21st Century* (see, for example, page 52). The idea of funding following the learner may well form a more important part of policy later in this Parliament, however, as the experimental work on Individual Learning Accounts is evaluated and there is an increased drive for individuals to invest in their own lifelong learning.

Key issues emerging from New Labour's approach to higher education

From what has been discussed above, we would suggest that New Labour has begun to address some of the immediate financial and other problems facing the higher education sector in the late 1990s. In this it has been guided by many of the detailed recommendations set out in the Dearing Report on higher education. However, like this report, New Labour's policies for higher education might be criticized as a series of initiatives which lack overall coherence. More importantly, it is hard to detect a clear vision of the future of higher education in this country or of a strategy for attaining this vision. It is therefore not yet evident whether New Labour sees higher education as a single sector with a single national mission or as a conglomeration of competing institutions with different missions tailoring their offer to particular niche markets. As described earlier in the chapter, there are the beginnings of a more planned approach to the sector at the regional level through RDAs, but these agencies are still at a very early stage of development and their role in relation to higher education or other regional bodies is not yet evident. The national steer, beyond the imperative to widen participation and to support the lifelong learning mission, is unclear and there is no apparent planning mechanism beyond the use of rather weak funding levers.

Perhaps a clear national strategy for higher education is impossible in the current national and international context, but it does leave a number of fundamental questions unanswered. For example, is higher education a particular stage in lifelong learning, which might be offered in any number of contexts, or is it a particular set of institutions? There appears to be an assumption that higher education institutions have a role to play in researching and disseminating new knowledge as well as in teaching, but it is not clear whether the balance between these two will be the same for all institutions. Which is more important – widening participation and responding to the needs and demands of learners or building an international reputation for research?

There is a recognition of the power of external factors, such as globalization, national and international economies and information and communication technologies, to affect the role of higher education in the future and yet there is no clear indication of how either the Government or individual institutions should respond to these factors beyond competing with others at a national and international level. Does the increasing ratio of private to public funding in higher education have an impact on the sector's power to act as an observer and critic of society? Is it simply up to the market to determine the shape of both higher education and individual higher education institutions, or does the state have a fundamental stake and role in the system?

New Labour's current policies for higher education do not, we would suggest, provide many answers to these difficult but essential questions. New Labour does have a central message – higher education institutions should support the drive for an inclusive approach to lifelong learning to achieve employability at the individual level and economic competitiveness at the national level – but this does not constitute a vision or strategy for higher education as a whole. Moreover, it does not take into account the history and traditions of different parts of the sector or the effects of the current national and international market in education and training.

Building a longer-term strategy

In this chapter we have examined New Labour's approach to both further and higher education. We would argue that more than any other government before, this administration has stressed the importance of integration between the further and higher education sectors because of its desire to promote the concept of lifelong learning. Baroness Blackstone's appointment as Minister with responsibility for both sectors and David Blunkett's statement in his letter to Lord Davies at the beginning of *Further Education for the New Millennium* (DfEE, 1998o) are both testimony to this position: 'Further and Higher Education are integral to the whole of our lifelong agenda, and the Government's new vision can only be fulfilled if both sectors respond to the challenge of creating a learning society.'

The central message to both further and higher education is the same – widening participation in high quality education and training is the way to economic prosperity and a more equal society. Considerable new money has been promised to both sectors to support them in this mission, with further education, the major beneficiary, being given £725 million more in the period 1999–2001. This will certainly go some way towards solving the critical financial crisis in the two sectors and will stabilize the position of many further education colleges. There is no doubt, therefore, of the seriousness of New Labour's commitment to the lifelong learning project and its plans for both sectors in the short term – expand and recruit from new sections of the population.

However, there is less clarity about the Government's longer-term plans for either sector. As we have indicated above, there is very little in New Labour's policy documents so far about the future strategic role of either further or higher education and even less about the future shape of the post-compulsory education and training system as a whole, beyond some tentative indications of a future regional agenda. Within the current market-led environment this could, as we have suggested earlier, lead to duplication of provision, loss of specialist provision or even unproductive competition and conflict between the further and higher education sectors around Level 3 and Level 4 provision which could, in turn, restrict student choice and access. Moreover, it will almost certainly lead to mission confusion, particularly for many higher education institutions which have not traditionally seen widening participation as high on their agenda.

Widening participation in the post-compulsory education and training system is a laudable first aim and long overdue, but it is only a first aim and it needs to be supported by clear longer-term goals for both further and higher education separately and for the shape of the post-compulsory education and training system as a whole. Otherwise, there is the danger that we could simply drift into a US-style system with all its attendant problems of low quality and qualifications inflation.

We would argue that there is a need for the Government actively to engage in a debate about the future shape of the UK post-compulsory education system for the 21st century and then to articulate clearly its longer-term strategy. We would suggest that the debate might begin by looking at five areas.

First, New Labour should consider what the primary missions are for both the further and higher education sectors, especially around Level 4 vocational and degree provision.

Second, there is the whole issue of low-quality provision in both further and higher education. This is an area which the Government has begun to address, but which needs further attention if its goals of economic prosperity and equity are to be met.

Third, there is the thorny issue of the relationship between the education and training system and the labour market. More particularly, there is a need to clarify the role which employers and trade unions should play in the system, both in terms of their complementary involvement in skills development and in the way they recognize and use qualifications and qualified employees.

Fourth, we would argue that both further and higher education need a strong national infrastructure or framework within which to operate in the 21st century. This should include, for example, a common qualifications framework across the whole post-compulsory education and training system and common quality assurance and funding systems (see Chapter 6 and 7).

Finally, we see an important role for the new RDAs, working within a strong national framework for the education and training system as a whole, in supporting all providers and users in a particular area to collaborate over the development of high quality learning opportunities in a wide range of different contexts.

Notes

1 This strategy, which combines a number of initiatives related specifically to the support of 16–19-year-olds, is discussed in more detail in Chapter 4.
2 This initiative, together with employee development schemes and IiP, is discussed in more detail in Chapter 2.
3 The New Deal forms the subject of Chapter 3.

6

Curriculum and Qualifications Reform from 14+

The context for New Labour's approach to qualifications reform

For the last 20 years and particularly over the last decade, there has been a continuing debate about the need for reform of the post-16 qualifications system in the UK. Around 30 major documents on this subject have been published by a wide range of academics, policy makers, think tanks, professional associations, government departments and political parties (eg Finegold *et al*, 1990; Royal Society, 1991; Labour Party, 1992, 1996; National Commission on Education, 1993, 1995; Scottish Office, 1994; Liberal Democrats, 1993; AfC *et al*, 1994; NAHT, 1995; Dearing, 1996; Hodgson and Spours, 1997b; SCAA and NCVQ, 1997; Pearce and Hillman, 1998). The reports reflect a widespread professional and political consensus that the qualifications system should be improved by making it more flexible, inclusive and unified. Many who criticize the current system highlight its narrowness, comparing it unfavourably with other European countries; its social and educational divisiveness; its complexity; and the fact that it contributes to low levels of achievement for 18 and 19-year-olds in this country.

During this period, there has been a difference between the way that both qualifications reform and debates about reform have taken place in Scotland, on the one hand, and in England, Wales and Northern Ireland on the other. Scotland has been on a strategic path of development towards fundamental reform of its 16–19 qualifications system since the mid-1980s and the debates which have taken place around this reform have been less politicized than in England, Wales and Northern Ireland (Howieson *et al*, 1997). Both the recent Conservative Government and New Labour have allowed developments in Scotland to take place in a way which would be inconceivable in England, Wales and Northern Ireland because of the political sensitivity around A levels in these three latter countries. Since qualifications reform is taking such a different and distinctive path in Scotland and New Labour is largely following the course set by the previous administration in relation to Scotland, we do not intend to discuss developments in that country in any detail in this chapter. Here we focus primarily on what is happening in England, Wales and Northern Ireland. We also consider New Labour's approach to qualifications and curriculum reform from 14+, rather than simply for 16–19-year-olds, because what happens to reforms for this latter age group is intimately bound up with developments in the last two years of compulsory schooling in England, Wales and Northern Ireland. It is also becoming increasingly important to widen discussions of qualifications reform to the whole age range in the light of the growing focus on lifelong learning.

Throughout the early 1990s, substantial movement towards a more unified and flexible qualifications system was taking place in a gradual but planned manner in Scotland, culminating in the publication of *Higher Still* in 1994 (Scottish Office, 1994). However, reform in England, Wales and Northern Ireland at this time was moving in a rather different direction. The introduction of a formalized triple-track qualifications system based on A levels, GNVQs and NVQs, as a result of the White Paper *Education and Training for the 21st Century* (DfE/ED/WO, 1991), made the system in England, Wales and Northern Ireland more divided and less flexible (Spours, 1993). Not surprisingly, the calls for reform of the qualifications system, rather than being satisfied by these moves, intensified. By 1995, against the background of revised National Targets for Education and Training and increasing evidence of poor performance of the triple-track qualifications system, there was a recognition by the Conservative Government that a more extensive review of the post-16 qualifications system was required.

As a result, Sir Ron Dearing, fresh from his work on the National Curriculum, was appointed to: 'consider and advise the Secretaries of State for Education and Employment and for Wales on ways to strengthen, consolidate and improve the framework of 16–19 qualifications' (Dearing, 1996: 1). However, he was also given a very constrained brief which included 'maintaining the rigour' of A levels and continuing 'to build on the current developments' of GNVQ. The kind of radical reforms which many of those who had been pressing for changes to the qualifications system since the early 1990s had hoped for, were thus effectively thwarted from the beginning of the review and consultation process. Nevertheless, a strong consensus for moving towards a more flexible, inclusive and unified system continued to build up during the period of the Dearing review and appeared to gain support from New Labour in 1996 when it published *Aiming Higher: Labour's proposals for the reform of the 14–19 curriculum* (Labour Party, 1996b) just one week prior to the publication of the final Dearing Report itself.

Qualifications system problems

By the time New Labour came to office in 1997, it inherited a post-16 education and training system which was in stasis in terms of growth in participation and, to a lesser extent, achievement. Levels of full-time post-16 participation, after rising dramatically for some years, had begun to decline and achievement rates at GCSE and at A level were still increasing but had slowed down (Spours, 1995, 1998). The numbers of students dropping out of full-time courses were rising, completion rates in GNVQs, which were meant to boost participation and achievement, were very poor (FEDA/IOE/Nuffield, 1997) and the occupationally-focused NVQ qualifications, introduced a decade earlier, continued to be the focus of constant criticism (Robinson, 1996). Moreover, the numbers of young people gaining no qualifications at 16+ still remained high and evidence was beginning to emerge of a widening gap between high and low attainers (QCA, 1998a). This polarized position was giving rise to increasing concerns about problems associated with disaffection and social exclusion (Pearce and Hillman, 1998; Hodgson, 1999). GCSE, which had initially done a great deal to increase the numbers of learners gaining access to post-16 study in the early 1990s (Gray, Jesson and Tranmer, 1993), was, by the mid-1990s, beginning to be criticized for creating a barrier to progression for the many young people unable to gain the necessary A*–C grades to obtain entry to A level or GNVQ Advanced Level programmes (Cockett and Callaghan, 1996).

There was an expectation, therefore, that when New Labour came into power one year after the publication of Dearing's *Review of Qualifications for 16–19-Year-Olds* (1996), it would build on those recommendations within the report which chimed with its vision expressed in *Aiming Higher*. There was an anticipation that it would make moves to bring about the unified qualifications system which had been part of Labour Party policy since the early 1990s (Labour Party, 1992a) in order to tackle the kind of problems it had inherited from the Conservatives.

We will argue in this chapter that the initial reforms which New Labour has proposed following the *Qualifying for Success* (DfEE, 1997a) consultation (eg the rather tentative changes to A levels, GNVQs and NVQs and the introduction of Key Skills and Entry Level qualifications) mark a small first step in the direction of the more flexible, coherent and inclusive 14–19 qualifications system described in *Aiming Higher*. On the other hand, the fact that the Government has been so lukewarm about the development of an overarching certificate at advanced level (DfEE, 1998f) and that there is still undisguised anxiety about reforming either GCSEs or A levels, gives rise to concern about New Labour's commitment to the vision of a coherent and unified 14+ qualifications system. Some indication of the issues to which New Labour has been responding can be illustrated through a brief discussion of recent key background debates on qualifications reform.

Key debates about qualifications reform during the 1990s

A continuous debate about qualifications reform has been underway in England and Wales for over two decades. This debate has been influenced by two factors in particular – how to respond to rising levels of participation and, in this process, how to avoid reforming A levels (Howieson *et al*, 1997; Spours, 1999).

During the 1990s, there have been several specific strands to the debate about qualifications reform which have in one way or another contributed to New Labour's own thinking prior to the 1997 general election. First, like many others who have proposed reform measures, including Sir Ron Dearing, New Labour has tended to focus on the problems of A levels, because of their top-down effect on the 14+ curriculum. This focus on advanced level has led to a relative neglect of qualifications reform at other levels. Only when in office did New Labour turn its attention to the 14-16 age range because of the growing importance of strategies for educational and social inclusion (see Pearce and Hillman, 1998). Second, New Labour strongly associated itself with the growing number of proposals for a more flexible and unified qualifications system from 14+ (Labour Party, 1992b, 1996b). It tried to incorporate features of different unifying approaches – notably 'baccalaureate' proposals (eg Finegold *et al*, 1990; NCE, 1995; NAHT, 1995) and those advocating unitization (eg AfC *et al*, 1994). Third, New Labour joined in the criticism of the newly-introduced NVQs and GNVQs which spanned the political spectrum. In 1996, a number of leading academics, with quite different positions on qualifications reform, signed a common letter to the *Financial Times* criticizing competence-based vocational qualifications (Senker, 1996). Central to the argument of these critics was the relationship between competence-based methods, excessive assessment bureaucracy and variability of standards. These concerns were to be echoed in New Labour's *Aiming Higher*. A fourth aspect of the debate, which was largely focused on the academic and vocational divide at advanced level, was the problem of how to pace reform. By the mid-1990s, proposals for reform had moved away from radical blueprints (eg Finegold *et al*, 1990; Royal Society, 1991; NCE, 1995) to phased strategies for change (Richardson *et al*, 1995; Young and Spours, 1998). It was not surprising that the concept of phased change was eagerly embraced by New Labour as it grappled with the problem of working with a radical unified vision in a fragmented qualifications system which had shown itself to be historically resistant to fundamental change.

New Labour's approach to 14–19 curriculum and qualifications reform

As we have already indicated, these debates have had an important effect on New Labour's approach to qualifications reform. We will argue that their different aspects have affected different phases of Labour policy. In the period 1992–96, the Labour Party identified itself closely with a unified qualifications strategy (Labour Party, 1992a, 1996b). Immediately prior to the election, in the form of its manifesto commitments (Labour Party,

1997), and in government, New Labour has narrowed the focus of reform in this area to a limited range of initiatives (eg broadening A levels, upgrading vocational qualifications and introducing Key Skills) within what has been termed a 'linked system' (Raffe *et al*, 1997). In government, New Labour appears to have become much more cautious than in opposition and is still debating how to move forward in this area.

In this section of the chapter we first examine New Labour's approach to curriculum and qualifications reform from 14+ prior to the election. We then describe some of the policies which it has put into place since coming to power. Finally, we examine how these policies might develop in the future.

Aiming Higher

In opposition, as we have indicated above, New Labour allied itself with those who argued for a more flexible, unified and comprehensive qualifications system, criticizing the current system for being too narrow and specialist and causing problems of 'low participation and achievement rates, high drop-out rates, variable standards and restricted scope for broad-based study' (Labour Party, 1996b: 1). New Labour also saw the introduction of an 'Advanced Diploma' as being the major vehicle for achieving curriculum and qualifications reform for 14–19-year-olds. In *Aiming Higher* the need for reform in this area is seen as 'urgent', the consensus for reform is recognized and there is a clear link made between the curriculum for 14–16-year-olds and that for 16–19-year-olds and beyond.

The Conservatives are criticized for 'resisting constructive proposals for reform' and for introducing change which 'was piecemeal and uncoordinated'. New Labour's plans are, in the first instance, to 'develop a post-16 curriculum structure that provides high standards, flexibility and the opportunity to combine different areas of study' and then, in the longer term to develop a '14–19+ curriculum that secures high performance and excellence for all ...(through) an integrated and unified approach which breaks down the historic and artificial divide that has existed for too long in this country between academic and vocational learning' (Labour Party, 1996b: 2).

The main argument in this document is for the broadening of A level programmes and the raising of standards in vocational programmes, combined with the bringing together of all 16–19 qualifications in a modular form under a single credit framework. It is suggested that all advanced level education should be recognized by the award of an Advanced Diploma at Level 3. *Aiming Higher* sees New Labour's proposals for reform being nationally co-ordinated by a single qualifications and regulatory body, the National Qualifications Council, within which a Core Skills Unit would be established to develop the 'core studies' which would form an integral part of all 14–19-year-old learners' programmes.

There is also brief mention in this document of the need for a 'more sophisticated range of assessment modes' and the importance of all learners having access to impartial careers advice and guidance, community studies, knowledge and understanding of the world of work and active citizenship.

No precise time-scale is attached to any of the reform proposals but, as indicated above, the need for reform in this area is seen as 'urgent' and there is a suggestion of a phased approach which initially addresses the need for a 'high-standard, flexible post-16 curriculum' and later develops 'a coherent and integrated 14–19+ curriculum' (page 17). It was widely interpreted that *Aiming Higher* was part of a 10-year strategy of change spanning two parliaments in which a coherent and integrated 14–19 system is attempted in a second term of office (Spours and Young, 1996).

New Labour in government and Qualifying for Success

In its 1997 election manifesto, New Labour decided that its priorities for qualifications reform would be to 'support broader A levels, upgrade vocational qualifications underpinned by rigorous standards and key skills' (Labour Party, 1997). This represented a narrowing of its objectives outlined in *Aiming Higher*: there is no mention of a single framework, an Advanced Diploma or a coherent 14–19+ system. It was assumed by those familiar with New Labour's policy approach that these more ambitious policies had not been abandoned, but would be addressed later, if the Labour Government succeeded in achieving a second term of office (Hodgson, Spours and Young, 1998).

We will argue that New Labour's cautious approach to qualifications reform to date has been framed by two factors. First, it has had to respond to the reform agenda, in the form of the Dearing *Review of Qualifications for 16–19-Year-Olds* (1996), the Beaumont Review of 100 leading NVQs/SVQs (1995) and the Capey Review of GNVQ Assessment (1996), inherited from the Conservative Government. These reviews were seen as broadly helpful because they represent attempts to take a more pragmatic approach to qualifications arrangements compared with those of the 1991 White Paper *Education and Training for the 21st Century*. The second reason for New Labour's caution in the area is more overtly political. Despite the gradualist and staged approach towards the development of a unified system outlined in *Aiming Higher*, this was still seen as too explicit for New Labour's policy agenda for a first parliament, because it might be interpreted as a long-term threat to A levels. However, the narrower manifesto commitments could be seen as taking the first tentative steps outlined in *Aiming Higher*, while being linked more overtly to maintaining educational standards rather than to overcoming the academic/vocational divide.

What the new Government inherited was a reform process that was well underway. However, the Dearing proposals were already running into technical and presentational difficulties, particularly around some of the more radical reforms associated with changes to A level syllabuses, the introduction of Key Skills qualifications and the design of the so-called 'Dearing Diploma'.

New Labour's immediate response was to put the Dearing reform process on hold on the grounds that the implementation process had been rushed and time was needed to reappraise the situation (DfEE, 1997e). The Government decided to launch a further round of review and consultation based on its own policy document *Qualifying for Success* (DfEE, 1997a). At the same time, it indicated a move in the direction of unification by bringing the Schools Curriculum and Assessment Authority (the body responsible for the regulation of academic qualifications) and the National Council for Vocational Qualifications (the body responsible for approving and developing vocational awards) together into a single regulatory body, the Qualifications and Curriculum Authority (QCA), and by rationalizing the major academic and vocational awarding bodies into three leading organizations (DfEE, 1997f, 1997g). The unification of regulatory and awarding bodies was not in itself a New Labour innovation because this move too, reflected recommendations in the Dearing Report. Moreover, these two moves towards a more unified system could also be seen as an evolutionary development following the successful formation of a unified ministry for both education and employment – the DfEE (Spours *et al*, 1998).

In its *Qualifying for Success* consultation paper on 16–19 qualifications, the newly-elected Labour Government proposed to break A levels into two three-unit blocks (AS and A2); to make changes to GNVQs to bring them more into line with A levels, in terms of grading and structure; to introduce Key Skills qualifications; and 'to work in the longer term towards an overarching certificate, building on the Dearing proposals for National Certificates and a National Advanced Diploma' (DfEE, 1997a: 23). These proposals were designed to create more common features between advanced level qualifications and to break large qualifications down into smaller blocks which could be more flexibly combined into mixed and broader learner programmes.

Due to the complex issues which had to be investigated and resolved, it was thought that the overarching certificate would not be implemented before 2001. However, there was an indication that the eventual implementation of an overarching certificate at advanced level might be followed by the introduction of certification at intermediate level.

The *Qualifying for Success* document was greeted with muted support by both academics and practitioners (eg IOE, 1997). In general, there was support for many of the proposals put forward, but a concern about some of the language used in relation to the reform process as a whole, and in particular in relation to A levels and assessment, where the desire to maintain 'rigour' and 'standards' seemed to militate against any real change. There was particular anxiety too about how any of the reforms might be implemented in practice (for instance, encouraging A level students to study more subjects), unless some form of incentive or compulsion was used. However, it was very unclear whether the new government was committed to this approach.

Baroness Blackstone's own response to QCA's report on the *Qualifying for Success* consultation process (DfEE, 1998e) was much more cautious than one might have expected from a Government committed to qualifications reform of the type described in *Aiming Higher* and, arguably, more cautious than might have been suggested by the *Qualifying for Success* consultation document itself. Her letter to Sir William Stubbs, Chair of QCA, was a mix of radical analysis of the limits of A levels, together with modest proposals for their reform through the proposed new AS/A2 blocks. She described current advanced level study as overspecialized and inflexible and observed that young people are taught for less time and have narrower programmes than in other European countries. Accompanying the proposals for smaller A level and GNVQ blocks was a series of tough measures – limits on the number of module resits, the limit on coursework assessment was raised from only 20 per cent to 30 per cent and there was a suggestion that advanced level study should normally be restricted to two years. This was clearly an effort to balance the reform of A level structure with measures which could be seen to be preserving standards, so as to be able to fend off accusations from the right-wing press of diluting A levels.

At the same time, it was recognized that there was 'growing support for exploring' both a unit-based credit system and overarching certification. Despite this, however, the Minister was of the opinion that a number of 'conceptual and practical' difficulties had to be confronted and that QCA 'should examine all the issues thoroughly before offering further advice'. Baroness Blackstone also stated that this advice should take account of the views of all key interest groups and the readiness of institutions to respond effectively to whatever changes might be envisaged. Despite all the consultation that had already taken place, it was suggested that a date for implementation would not be set until further research and development work had been done.

Reform measures and proposals following Qualifying for Success

Following the *Qualifying for Success* consultation process, the Government has focused qualifications reform in four main areas. We will briefly outline their key proposals and indicate some of the more specific debates in relation to each. Our analysis is, however, selective and some detailed proposals have been omitted on the grounds that they do not have significant whole-system implications.

Changes to A levels and the introduction of smaller qualification blocks

One of the most important new proposals is to split all A levels into two three-unit blocks – AS and A2 – and to encourage learners to broaden their advanced level programmes by taking up to five AS or equivalent blocks in the first year of study, rather than the traditional three A levels. Under this reform, students will be able to achieve a three-unit AS in the first year and a three-unit A2 in the second year, thereby achieving a full A level over two years. Study in both AS and A2 is at advanced level, though the standard of the AS is below that of a full A level, and two AS levels (on paper at least) will count as one full A level. These A level reforms will be launched in September 2000.

As part of the *Qualifying for Success* consultation, there was a debate about the size and level of the three-unit AS block. Strong representations were made from the teaching profession for the AS to be two rather than three units in size to encourage more learners to broaden their study. This would also allow the AS to lie between Levels 2 and 3 so as to create a more gradual slope of progression (JACG, 1997). These proposals were rejected on the grounds first, that three-unit blocks were deemed the minimum size of qualification required to maintain coherence of study and second, that the proposed two-unit block might not establish credibility as a qualification in its own right. The idea of introducing a new level between GCSE and A level was viewed as too complex and it would give mixed messages about maintaining A level standards.[1]

The result is the scheduled introduction of a three-unit AS qualification block which is probably too big to encourage many learners to broaden their study voluntarily through taking more subjects. This may have already been recognized by those who advise Ministers because now there is less talk of learners typically taking five subjects in the first year. Moreover, the issue of the standard of the AS block remains complex. In some subjects, the AS will be easier than the A2. However, the AS will be regarded overall as being of A level standard. Nevertheless, these factors, which contribute to the lingering confusion about the level of the AS, may actually improve the possibility of progression within A levels. In this respect, the AS may come to more closely resemble the Scottish Higher.

Our own research with a number of local authorities over the last year suggests that only a small minority of schools or colleges will offer a significantly broader provision in the first year of an A level course and only a small minority of students may opt for this pattern of study. This is because there are fears both about what currency the new AS will have with higher education providers and employers and about the timetabling and resourcing of these broader types of study programme. Unless there are strong incentives to encourage institutions to do otherwise, the initial signs are that the broadening of the general education track through the introduction of these A level reforms will not be significant.

Alongside these reforms to A levels, there are proposals to split GNVQs into smaller six-unit or three-unit blocks in order to encourage learners to broaden their advanced level study programmes through the combination of smaller A level and GNVQ qualification blocks. More optimistic messages are being received from schools and colleges about the potential role of these smaller GNVQ blocks for encouraging the mixing of general and vocational study. However, if this is the only significant broadening pattern that takes place, there is a danger that it will be associated with the lower end of the A level cohort.

It looks, therefore, as if the broadening of advanced level study through learners using the new smaller qualification blocks to take up more subjects will rest on the strength of external incentives – funding regimes and resourcing, UCAS points and university acceptance and pressure from inspection regimes. In the longer term, we believe that the development of overarching certification will provide the strongest incentive for schools and colleges to broaden advanced level study.

Key Skills

The Government is committed to the introduction of Key Skills and would like to see these being taken by all learners from 14+. To this end, it has set about creating a single qualification to assess achievement in the Key Skills of Communication, Application of Number and Information Technology at Levels 1, 2 and 3 (DfEE, 1999c).

While the inclusion of Key Skills in post-16 study is broadly supported by the education profession, a number of problems are emerging with the Government's approach. First, its emphasis on external as well as internal assessment has made it more difficult for schools and colleges to implement the Key Skills pilots because of the increased burden of assessment. Moreover, those in the workplace have found the element of external assessment unhelpful (QCA, 1998b). Second, the Government makes a clear distinction between the 'first' three Key Skills – Communication, Application of Numbers and Information Technology – and the wider Key Skills of Improving Own Learning and Performance, Problem Solving and Working With Others. While a specific national qualification has been designed for the former, the latter are not being given the same treatment. However unintentionally, this gives a clear signal that the wider Key Skills are not perceived to be as important as the first three, despite their widespread support among employers and the education profession. Finally, while the Government is strongly committed to Key Skills for 14–19-year-olds, they will not be mandatory. Like the other *Qualifying for Success* reforms, their uptake will be in the hands of schools, colleges and employers offering Modern Apprenticeships who will be influenced, in turn, by higher education and the wishes of learners themselves.

Upgrading vocational qualifications and consistency within the national qualifications framework

GNVQs are being made 'stronger' by changes to their mode of assessment, including a revised grading system (aligned with A levels), by externally-set assignments and by revised Key Skill units. NVQs are being reformed in consultation with National Training Organizations with an emphasis on flexibility, rationalization and closer alignment with other vocational awards (QCA, 1999). (A further discussion of NVQs is contained in Chapter 4.)

The strengthening of vocational qualifications through external assessment and greater standardization can be seen as a means of expanding the national qualifications framework while, at the same time, avoiding diluting standards. It brings vocational qualifications more into line with general qualifications through the medium of external assessment, thereby making them more credible. This approach to vocational qualifications is very much a response to problems arising from the experimentation of the previous government with competence-based awards and with the longer-term problem of low status for vocational qualifications and curricula in this country.

New Labour, however, has as yet to map out a forward-looking approach to this area which is probably most in need of further reform. The debate still focuses on either the importance of external assessment or the need for occupational competence. Much less emphasis, if any, has been given to the need for 'skills for the future' (currently more associated with the wider Key Skills), for new ways of combining knowledge and skill and for innovative ways of combining learning and work at Levels 3 and above. As we have explained in previous chapters, New Labour has so far split its approach to reform between promoting access and social inclusion with a focus on Levels 1 and 2 and preserving standards at Level 3. The more forward-looking debates are currently confined to research on the overarching certificate at advanced level and proposals for unitization in vocational qualifications.

The overarching certificate at advanced level, unitization and a 14+ approach to the national qualifications framework

The more radical debates about developing an overarching certificate at advanced level, introducing unitization and credit and creating a qualifications system as a progression ladder from 14+ are significant for several reasons. First, they are reflections of a widespread professional consensus on how the qualifications system should develop, which emerged during the 1990s and which were also supported in *Aiming Higher*. Second, these approaches have been developed in Scotland through *Higher Still* (Scottish Office, 1994) and in Wales through CREDIS, the Welsh lifelong learning Green Paper (Welsh Office, 1998) and the Welsh Baccalaureate (Jenkins and David, 1996). Third, they are not part of the reforms implemented under *Qualifying for Success*. Instead they are being researched, discussed and debated separately and no precise timetable has been set for their implementation. The key question is whether New Labour wants to see these measures properly researched, debated and implemented in a staged and well-planned way in a second Parliament, or whether political caution in this area has diminished its appetite to such an extent that it has abandoned a long-term vision of qualifications and curriculum reform from 14+.

In May 1998, the regulatory bodies in England, Wales and Northern Ireland published a research specification for 'An Overarching Certificate at Advanced Level' (QCA/CCEA/ACCAC, 1998) and work is currently progressing on the design of such a certificate. At this time, it is possible that the

QCA's research report to Ministers on an overarching certificate at advanced level may propose that all students at this level should take some sort of core curriculum as well as specialist qualifications. However, both the QCA Board and Ministers have yet to consider and to comment on this proposal.[2]

There are three possible outcomes with regard to an overarching certificate at advanced level. The first is that such a certificate is launched early in the next Parliament, for example in 2002.[3] This time-scale would broadly correspond to the staged approach to creating an Advanced Diploma outlined in *Aiming Higher*. Of all the possible options, this is the least likely because it would mean taking a more radical decision on advanced level reform during this Parliament. The Government has already decided on reforms at advanced level as a result of the *Qualifying for Success* consultation process and will want to wait and see whether these are taken up by schools and colleges.

A second possibility is that the Government abandons altogether the idea of an overarching certificate and confines its reforms to those currently being implemented under *Qualifying for Success*. This will probably not happen, but it is more likely than a commitment to its early implementation. The reason why the Government may keep the overarching certificate on the agenda is that it is not entirely confident that the *Qualifying for Success* reforms will, in themselves, bring about the desired broadening of advanced level study. Moreover, the Government has already taken the first step in moving beyond the narrow diet of A levels, GNVQs and NVQs by its commitment to 'Key Skills for all'. If, in addition to these, the Government decides that other curricular elements, such as citizenship, parenting or a work-related curriculum, are also desirable as part of the concept of a '16–19 entitlement curriculum',[4] a stage will soon be reached where it is necessary to encapsulate these additional elements and the smaller A level and GNVQ qualification blocks within a common certification framework. Viewed this way, some form of overarching certification is probably inevitable in the long run.

This brings us to the third and most likely option – a slow and evolutionary approach in which the Government pragmatically tests out the permissive *Qualifying for Success* reforms and brings in an overarching certificate at advanced level, when it is absolutely necessary and when it is politically safe to do so. In this case, the time-scale is more likely to be well into a second Parliament, possibly as late as 2005. This form of gradualism is entirely consistent with New Labour's voluntarist and cautious approach to other areas of post-compulsory education and training, as outlined in other chapters of this book.[5] The important distinction between a pragmatic evolutionary approach and a staged radical approach with an explicit end-point is discussed in the final part of this chapter.

New Labour's caution in relation to the overarching certificate is also reflected in its attitude towards unitization and credit accumulation. Following the *Qualifying for Success* consultation, the Government drew a distinction between the qualifications needs of younger and older learners (DfEE, 1998f) which implied that unit-based qualifications would be developed for adults, but not for 16–19-year-olds on full-time programmes of study. However, development work is being undertaken by QCA (1999) into creating more flexibility within the national qualifications framework which will apply to vocational qualifications. If this happens it will only be a matter of time before pressures will build for this approach to be applied to general qualifications which are in closer alignment with vocational qualifications as a result of *Qualifying for Success*. Moreover, the distinction between qualifications designed for younger and older learners does not apply in Scotland's *Higher Still* proposal, nor is it reflected in the Welsh Green Paper on lifelong learning. If, due to devolved Parliaments, both of these smaller 'home international' systems proceed down a more radical and modular road, longer-term pressure is likely to mount for England and Northern Ireland to move in a similar direction.

The third radical proposal outlined in *Aiming Higher* was the idea of a 14+ qualifications system to challenge the sharp divide at 16+ and to provide a latticework of progression for learners at all levels within the national qualifications framework. The concept of a 14+ continuum has been widely supported across the education profession since TVEI in the mid-1980s. Nearly all of the 30 qualifications reform proposals published during the 1990s have a 14+ perspective rather than a 16–19 concept of reform. More recently, the idea of a 14+ continuum has been linked to providing more effective ways of including disaffected young people within a progression-oriented curriculum (Pearce and Hillman, 1998).

These arguments have not been challenged by Government because Ministers know they make sense. However, the same caution which holds sway in other areas also dominates thinking on this issue. Creating a 14+ curriculum and qualifications system will mean thoroughly reappraising the role of GCSE which, with its hardening A*–C cut-off point, is increasingly seen as a barrier to improving levels of achievement by the bottom half of the age group (Cockett and Callaghan, 1997; Pearce and Hillman, 1998). It is unlikely that the current review of the National Curriculum at Key Stage 4 will do more than confirm the movement towards greater flexibility and opening up opportunities for the study of more vocational qualifications for 14–16-year-olds. Any fundamental review of provision at 14+, like the other more radical system proposals, will at best be considered the other side of the next election.

Assessing New Labour's approach to qualifications reform

So what is the reasoning behind New Labour's cautious approach to qualifications reform? We will suggest that there are four major factors – policy hierarchy; dependence on voluntary reform with limited external incentives; negative system pressures and the 'low-achievement conspiracy'; and evolutionary policy responding to different pressures, each of which is discussed briefly below.

Not a top policy priority

Despite the fact that the English, Welsh and Northern Irish education system is qualifications led (Wolf, 1992; Howieson *et al*, 1997) and qualifications are seen to be important (DfEE, 1997a), qualifications reform does not currently appear to be at the top of New Labour's policy hierarchy. The prime positions are occupied by raising school standards in the area of compulsory education, and the implementation of the New Deal and widening participation in post-compulsory education and training. We are not questioning these priorities; they are very understandable given the nature of the Conservative legacy. However, to place the reform of A levels lower down the political agenda may be unwise, because qualifications dictate so much educational behaviour in this country. If the qualifications system is not radically reformed, it is likely to remain a barrier to increasing both the levels and quality of achievement at 14+, which can be seen as part of New Labour's 'standards' agenda, and to hamper New Labour's aspirations to tackle social and educational exclusion by widening participation and achievement in lifelong learning for all sections of society.

Dependence on voluntary reform with limited external incentives

The second reason for caution is that New Labour believes that much can be achieved by permissive or voluntarist initiatives and that what they should be providing is opportunities for individual choice and access rather than reforming the underlying structure of the system supported by a strong framework of incentives. If schools and colleges make the choice to offer the reformed qualifications New Labour has proposed, and if learners decide to study them, then Government can be seen to be supporting breadth because that is what younger learners and their parents want. It is envisaged that the reforms described above will be supported by incentives such as inspection criteria, funding regimes and a reformed UCAS tariff. However, these have not been spelled out in detail yet and may, in any case, not be enough to alter post-16 provision in the majority of schools and colleges, particularly in the current marketized education and training system.

Negative system pressures and the 'low-achievement conspiracy'

Despite a widespread professional consensus for reform, there is growing evidence of an institutional reluctance to broaden the advanced level curriculum voluntarily. This is due to what we have termed the 'low-achievement conspiracy' in which a syndrome of market forces diminishes the appetite of schools and colleges to broaden the advanced level curriculum and reduces the desire or need for learners to undertake more demanding advanced level study programmes (Hodgson and Spours, 1998). By this we refer to the interrelationship between a casualized youth labour market which attracts advanced level learners from their studies; schools and colleges which are afraid to make additional demands of students in case they defect to another institution; less popular higher education institutions being prepared to make low grade offers for university entry, while the more popular will stick with traditional A levels; funding methodologies which lower course contact hours; and many students who, in this context, have little commitment to their studies and try to get by with the bare minimum. Government needs to become much more aware of the effect that marketized forces have on learner motivation and choices and the implications of this for voluntarist policies.

Evolutionary policy responding to different pressures

To reform in such a situation will demand a strong steer from Government. However, currently this does not appear to be the preferred strategy. Instead, New Labour is prepared to be subjected to pressures both from those seeking reform and from those wishing to preserve A levels and a divided system. The main reason for this positioning is the belief that the professional consensus in favour of a more flexible and unified system, referred to at the beginning of this chapter, is too far ahead of public opinion (Spours, 1999) which knows where it is with A levels (Smithers, 1998). A slow and evolutionary process of change is seen, therefore, as the safest way forward.

The main difficulty with the Government's cautious strategy is that it may not effectively deliver its declared goals. The *Qualifying for Success* reforms are in the hands of schools and colleges who, in a market environment, are themselves under the influence of both higher education providers, employers and learners. Given the pressures which we have described above, they may well ignore the reforms and continue to offer a narrow A level or GNVQ diet, unless there are strong incentives for them to do otherwise.

The challenge of building a 14–19 curriculum and qualifications system for the 21st century

The consequences of New Labour's current approach to qualifications reform

After over a decade of debate about the need for curriculum and qualifications reform for 14–19-year-olds, the system in England, Wales and Northern Ireland has adapted but not changed in any fundamental sense. The most basic process of change has been one of system expansion rather than rationalization, with the addition of new awards, such as GNVQs, in response to rising levels of participation. This can be seen, however, as a form of divisive expansion leaving the qualifications system more complicated with an increase in different types of qualifications. New Labour is continuing this logic with the addition of the new Key Skills qualifications. At the same time, the *Qualifying for Success* reform process is trying to create a more consistent set of standards across the national qualifications framework, propelled largely by the role of external assessment.

Scotland has taken a different path of development as a result of the gradual reform process starting with the Scottish Action Plan in the mid-1980s, through the Howie Committee of 1992 and then the decision to implement *Higher Still* in 1994 (Howieson *et al*, 1997). The Scottish road has been more unified with the formation of a single ladder consisting of both general and vocational modules or short courses across five levels. Originating with general and broad vocational qualifications, the *Higher Still* system is still being gradually expanded to take in SVQs/NVQs. The Scottish single modular ladder also aims to embrace qualifications for both younger and older learners, unlike the *Qualifying for Success* reforms in England, Wales and Northern Ireland. The Welsh, following the establishment of their own Assembly, will probably proceed down a similar path to that taken by Scotland, though the amount of cross-border higher education admissions traffic between Wales and England may act to slow this process (Young *et al*, 1998).

In comparison with Scotland, south of the border New Labour has not pursued an overt unified approach. Rather it has pursued a 'linkages' approach based on tough standards (Raffe *et al*, 1997). This involves retaining existing qualifications, but creating links between them to promote qualifications consistency, breadth of study and parity of esteem based on the culture of the academic track. Our analysis throughout this chapter suggests that this linkages strategy is a first step in the direction of a more unified system but is unstable in the longer run.

New Labour's evolutionary approach to qualifications reform is practical but piecemeal and somewhat backward-looking. It is essentially reactive to the Conservative legacy and reflects a historical preoccupation with academic learning. Instead of pursuing a unified strategy in which the whole system is based on a transparent ladder of progression (as in Scotland), new Labour has pursued two conflicting themes of 'rigour' and 'access'. This is leading to confusion, to new lines of division and creates a barrier to thinking about the development of a coherent and progressive 14+ system for the 21st century.

Extensive discussions with teachers, lecturers and employers over the last year suggest that many are genuinely confused by New Labour's strategy and the direction of qualifications reform. In this context, they are less likely to take the first steps of reform and take risks with their students because they do not know whether the new qualifications will take hold or what they are working towards. Moreover, the picture of a Government hanging on to A levels and GCSEs is creating a psychological and cultural barrier which makes it very difficult to consider what is really required for the future.

In addition, the Government has taken a position on qualifications standards which may compromise its own laudable aim of raising levels of achievement among wider sections of the cohort. Its strategy appears to be based on raising levels of literacy and numeracy lower down the system so that, in the longer run, learners can cope with the rigorous standards which have been maintained in post-14 qualifications. However, the problem with this approach is that it is potentially naïve because New Labour expects its literacy and numeracy strategy to drive up standards to such an extent that learners will be immune from the 'low achievement conspiracy' and all the system barriers we have described earlier in the chapter.

An agenda for staged reform

Given the analysis above, we suggest that New Labour shifts its qualification reform approach towards a more robust and future-oriented strategy which addresses system barriers and encourages higher levels of qualification attainment for all from 14+. We suggest that there are six areas for action.

First, New Labour should indicate its renewed commitment to *Aiming Higher* and this document's staged approach to a unified and flexible qualifications system from 14+. This does not run counter to the reforms currently being implemented following *Qualifying for Success*. Rather, adopting a staged approach with a clearly stated end-point can be seen as a way of strengthening and clarifying the proposed reforms precisely because they are seen as a first step. This allows schools, colleges and employers to anticipate the future by gradually putting into place some of the building blocks of a 14+ curriculum and qualifications framework.

Second, New Labour should clearly signal its intention to build a 14+ rather than a 16+ qualifications and curriculum framework. This will require a review of the role of GCSE which, as we have indicated earlier in this chapter, has now become a major barrier to progression and achievement for the lower part of the age cohort.

Third, New Labour should commit itself to the implementation of overarching certification at advanced level and then, as appropriate, at lower levels. An overarching certificate at advanced level will help to secure the breadth of study which has been tentatively addressed through the *Qualifying for Success* reforms. However, we see the main function of the further development of overarching certification as providing a framework for considering a 'curriculum of the future'. Within this broad aim, overarching certification would support the role of the wider Key Skills and the type of learning required both to improve employability and to link the post-14 curriculum with the concept of citizenship in a rapidly changing world.

Fourth, it will be important to ensure that any overarching certification encompasses learning in the workplace. Elsewhere in this book we have argued that this is an area which has been relatively neglected in the debates about qualifications reform. New Labour should redress the balance by stressing that learners not only require breadth in terms of subject knowledge, but that there is also an important role for applied knowledge and skill and that these should become part of all learners' programmes. Moreover, there is a need to develop the concept of 'vocational specialization' which embraces both theory and application. It is our opinion that there are the beginnings of this approach in some of the well-respected traditional vocational qualifications, but that this concept has been neglected in the more recently-developed competence-based vocational qualifications.

Fifth, while New Labour's distinction between the needs of younger and older learners is justifiable on the grounds that one group is going through a process of 'formation' and the other is building on prior knowledge and experience, we do not think that this warrants an entirely different qualifications structure for the two groups. What is necessary is to build a 14+ curriculum and qualifications structure based on a flexible credit accumulation and transfer system which can accommodate more prescribed grouped awards for younger learners, as well as unitized qualifications and units to meet the needs of adult learners. This we would see as a genuine move in the direction of an 'all-through system' to support lifelong learning.

Finally, one of the major aspects of New Labour's approach which we have criticized in this chapter and elsewhere in the book is its reliance on voluntarist measures to bring about reform. The idea of a common framework from 14+ can be seen as the creation of a level playing field, but this will still require a framework of incentives in order to ensure that new and innovative combinations of study are recognized by end-users such as higher education providers. This, in turn, will help to encourage learners, schools and colleges to experiment with the new patterns of learning required for the future rather than adhering to the traditional pathways and approaches of the past.

We see these six areas of action, which, in our view, constitute a 'strong framework approach' to reform of the 14+ qualifications system, as forming an agenda in this area for New Labour's next term of office. This 'strong framework approach', which we apply across a range of policy areas in education and training, is explored further in Chapter 7. What is important in this Parliament is to decide on this course of action as part of a staged strategy to reform, rather than pursuing the more traditional political strategy of 'policy adjustment' as a response to policy failure. As well as setting in motion the *Qualifying for Success* reforms, it is important that the Government begins now to secure the consensus for more radical whole-system reform in a second term of office.

Notes

1 This perspective on the *Qualifying for Success* reforms was gleaned from a series of interviews with government advisers and senior officials during 1997–98.
2 The authors are part of the Research Team developing a model of an overarching certificate at advanced level and this information is based on their work at the time of going to press.
3 This is the earliest possible implementation date given that in *Qualifying for Success* the Government said that it was most unlikely to implement an overarching certificate at advanced level before 2001.
4 The term '16–19 entitlement curriculum' is one which has been used in the Government's response to the Sixth Report from the Education and Employment Committee on Further Education (House of Commons, 1999).
5 As part of the research team working on the design of an overarching certificate at advanced level, the authors have been in discussion with officials and Ministers in relation to this Project. The final report from this project has yet to be completed and submitted to QCA for comment before being passed on to Ministers.

7

New Labour's Approach to Education and Training from 14+: The Need to Move from Weak to Strong Frameworks

Introduction

Throughout the last five chapters of this book we have discussed New Labour's approach to various aspects of policy for education and training from 14+. However, in order to understand New Labour's overall approach to this area, it is important to view it from the perspective of lifelong learning, embracing both compulsory and post-compulsory education and training. In the Introduction to this book we drew a distinction between New Labour's policy agendas for compulsory education and post-compulsory education and training.

Its policy agenda for compulsory schooling has been strongly centralist and *dirigiste*, directed to the central objective of raising standards, such that, among other things, the middle classes can have renewed confidence in the comprehensive state school system. This approach has been reflected in measures such as national numeracy and literacy strategies, which for the first time specify in detail the content and method of classroom teaching practices; a legislative overhaul of the roles and responsibilities of schools, local authorities and central government; the introduction of a core curriculum for initial teaching education; active support for a controversial inspection regime inherited from the Conservative administration; proposals to radically change teachers' terms and conditions; and new powers to replace 'failing' local education authorities with private organizations from a centrally approved list of providers.

New Labour's policy agenda for post-compulsory education and training, on the other hand, has been much more cautious, voluntarist and experimental. Exceptions to this norm have been rare. The most prominent and controversial have been the powers taken in the Teaching and Higher Education Act 1998 to limit the ability of higher education institutions to charge differential entry fees to students, and the introduction of a tough benefit regime in the New Deal.

In order to illustrate New Labour's approach in this area, in the first part of this chapter we draw together 10 overarching themes which we believe inform New Labour's policy approach to education and training from 14+. In the second part of the chapter we suggest that these themes have resulted in a 'weak framework' approach to policy which we relate to New Labour's focus on reform through initiatives and voluntarist action in a modified market. We go on to develop the concept of a 'strong framework' strategy which we relate to the need for structural reform of the education and training system as a whole. We argue that there will be increasing internal and external pressures for New Labour to develop stronger frameworks to tackle the system barriers which threaten to undermine their current initiatives designed to promote lifelong learning. The book thus concludes by laying out some tentative ideas for an agenda in this area for New Labour if it achieves a second term of office.

New Labour's emerging policy themes for education and training from 14+

In this section we draw on some of the more detailed debates which have been discussed in earlier chapters of the book in order to identify the 10 key themes which run through New Labour's policy approach to the education and training system from 14+. Alongside this brief analytical section we go on to look at the reasons for the emergence of these themes and to consider whether they constitute a Third Way policy approach.

Continuity and break

Despite the anti-Conservative rhetoric in many of New Labour's policy documents prior to the general election, as earlier chapters in this book have pointed out, one of the key overarching themes of New Labour's approach to education and training from 14+ is continuity with the previous administration's agenda in this area. We will suggest that there are possibly three reasons for this.

First, continuity reflects a pragmatic response to the Conservative policy legacy. It has to be remembered that New Labour did not enter office during the high water mark of market-led education and training policies under Margaret Thatcher's premiership, but in the more pragmatic and consultative era under Prime Minister John Major, when the Rt Hon Gillian Shephard was Secretary of State at the DfEE. The period just prior to New Labour's election could be characterized as one of consolidation and review in terms of education and training policy. The findings of the two Dearing Reviews (1995, 1996), the Capey Review of GNVQs (1995) and the

Beaumont Review of NVQs (1995) had already been reported and the Kennedy Committee (1997) and the National Committee of Inquiry into Higher Education (1997) were due to publish their recommendations. Moreover, the Conservatives had introduced Modern Apprenticeships in 1994 along with the formation of National Training Organizations. It is not surprising, therefore, that a new government, inheriting this legacy of large-scale consultations, recommendations and recent improvements in many of the key areas of post-compulsory education and training, was not prepared to reject these reforms and reviews outright (Hillman, 1998).

A second reason is that while New Labour inherited a pragmatic reform process, it also inherited severe system problems rooted in earlier market-led Conservative policies which, as earlier chapters of the book point out, had led to polarization of education and training opportunities and to social and educational exclusion. New Labour's first priority was, therefore, to tackle the immediate human problems of social exclusion rather than long-term underlying system problems. We have argued throughout the various chapters in this book that the Conservative legacy has had a major shaping effect on New Labour's education policy. Even those policies which are distinctly New Labour can be seen to be reacting to the Conservative legacy (eg New Deal).

A possible third reason for the continuity argument is that New Labour's policies reflect the type of consensus politics associated with the Third Way which actively attempts to steer a course between Thatcherite and social democratic ideas.

On closer analysis it appears that there might be an element of truth in all three positions, although we believe that there is more evidence for the first two than for the idea of a coherent Third Way approach to post-compulsory education and training. Later in this chapter we suggest that the idea of a Third Way in relation to education and training might embrace not one but two positions which we describe as 'weak' and 'strong' framework approaches. The former, we suggest, is largely a response to the Conservative legacy: the latter, in our conception, relates to a potential agenda for a second Parliament in which policy is less tied to the past and more focused on the future.

Despite our argument about New Labour's responsiveness to the Conservative legacy, at the level of political rhetoric and avowed intentions there is a strong sense of break which is marked in particular by an emphasis on social and education inclusion. But at the level of policy, particularly in relation to whole system approaches, there is still considerable continuity. The question we pose is whether this position will change over time and whether policies will move closer to the rhetoric in which New Labour charts out more fully its own agenda. In other words, is the current New Labour agenda 'a first base', and not the 'last word', as Tony Blair suggested in a recent speech at IPPR? (Blair, 1999).

A policy hierarchy

One of the clearest features of New Labour's overall approach to education and training is its development of a strong policy hierarchy. This is linked to its manifesto commitments (Labour Party, 1997) and based, in the case of the post-compulsory phase, on a specific selection of ideas from documents produced between 1993 and 1996. As in other areas of government, New Labour has focused its energy on delivering a small number of promises in its first Parliament as a basis for re-election to a second term. However, apart from the New Deal, post-compulsory education and training appears to have a relatively low ranking in the overall education policy hierarchy and has thus received less attention than compulsory education which carries greater political significance.

We see New Labour's development of a policy hierarchy both as a result of its reaction to the Conservative legacy and its desire to be re-elected by successfully delivering a limited number of key high-profile political objectives. This approach, however, can easily lead to policy dogma. This describes a situation in which policy issues are either on or off the current agenda, resulting in a lack of responsiveness and a fear of criticism or debate since the championing of certain issues which are 'off' the agenda is seen as a threat to the smooth implementation of the key objectives. The main problem with this approach is that it inhibits open debate and relies on a process of 'stealth' to achieve policy reform; a process eloquently illustrated by the current tortuous approach to qualifications reform described in Chapter 6.

Widening participation and tackling educational exclusion

Widening participation and tackling social and educational exclusion are more than a policy theme for New Labour. They have become a means of interpretation for all aspects of policy on post-compulsory education and training in this Parliament and are much more pervasive than even pre-election policy documents would have suggested. This is, therefore, an area in which New Labour has been very active in the early part of this Parliament. Initiatives such as the New Deal, New Start and Education Action Zones, alongside funding steers to encourage further and higher education to widen participation, can be seen as part of a desire to tackle the Conservative legacy of the 'lost generation', the socially marginalized and the long-term unemployed. As previous chapters have suggested, this approach is related to basic commitments to social inclusion, as well as to the specific conviction that sharply divided societies are neither prosperous nor competitive. Consequently, there is a need for redistribution of educational opportunities to address social division. In this sense, New Labour's approach might be seen as a continuation of system expansion, begun under the Conservatives, but with a new focus and direction.

Initiatives-led reform

One of the major characteristics of New Labour's approach in all areas of education and training policy, but particularly post-14, is initiatives-led reform (eg UfI, New Deal and ILAs). The reasons for this are also closely tied to the issue of the Conservative legacy. First, there is a desire to use pragmatic solutions swiftly to remediate problems facing those groups excluded from the Conservative expansion of the education and training system. Second, this approach may be associated with a Third Way orientation, insofar as initiatives are designed to avoid historical ideological baggage (eg ILAs instead of a levy and regulation). Third, there is a compelling drive to be seen to be doing something to fulfil election promises.

We have suggested in earlier chapters that initiatives-led reform, while radical and innovative, and with the potential to make a practical difference to the most excluded groups in society, has neither the power to change the structure of the education and training system as a whole, nor to alter its overall effectiveness.

Joined-up government

The setting up of the Social Exclusion Unit (SEU), which reports directly to the Prime Minister, and the introduction of the New Deal programme, which links education, training, employment and welfare, are both testimony to the Government's desire to pursue 'joined-up' thinking in relation to deep-rooted problems such as social exclusion and marginalization. This joined-up Government strategy indicates both a desire to improve policy co-ordination in order to tackle long-standing problems, but also addresses a perceived need to improve efficiency in public administration in order to avoid increasing taxes. As Tony Blair put it in his speech to the 10th Anniversary Conference of the Institute for Public Policy Research, a key tenet of the Third Way is the 'belief that how government spends, and on what, is as important as how much it spends' (Blair, 1999).

We will argue that joined-up thinking and cross-departmental co-ordination at the national level have been used to remediate complex social problems inherited from the Conservatives. However, they do not yet constitute the type of joined-up system which will be required to eliminate the barriers which currently prevent all learners, not just the most disadvantaged, from effective participation in lifelong learning.

Standards and system expansion

In the Introduction to this book we highlighted New Labour's preoccupation with educational standards. This appears to consist of two apparently contradictory approaches. First, there is a desire to *improve* standards in order to create a reputable state education system which will be attractive to parents, but in particular, to middle class parents: hence the emphasis on investment, strong inspection regimes, parental involvement and the basics of literacy and numeracy. The aim of the school standards drive is to ensure that more learners achieve a nationally defined standard in compulsory education.

However, in post-compulsory education and training, New Labour sees the importance of *maintaining* standards in order to counteract the claims that system expansion has led to a decline in standards. This approach helps to explain the desire to retain A levels, to improve vocational qualifications and to support traditional higher education institutions. The problem with this approach to post-compulsory education and training is that the emphasis on standards maintenance may result in policies that could depress levels of achievement (see Chapter 6). We will argue in the final part of this chapter that New Labour will need to be clearer on whether it wants to create greater access to achievement and to develop 'standards for the future', or whether it wants to adhere to traditional notions of standards inherited from its predecessors.

Centralization and voluntarism

New Labour's policies in the areas of education and training manifest a mix of centralization and voluntarism. The centralization, inherited from the Conservatives, is related to the unification of ministries and regulatory authorities, the formation of national funding bodies and a reduced role for local education authorities. At the same time, New Labour has emphasized the role of individuals investing in their education and training and has continued a voluntarist approach to the labour market, employers and to the post-compulsory curriculum.

New Labour has not, so far, reversed the centralizing tendencies it inherited from the Conservatives. However, there is a move in the direction of more devolved power to the regions through RDAs, although this is as yet undeveloped. There is also an increasing emphasis on voluntary local partnerships and collaboration. Later in the chapter we argue, like Pearce and Hillman (1998), that there is a need for the Government to move more strongly in the direction of devolving power to the regional level in order to provide a stronger framework for the type of regional and local collaboration required to support individual learners.

Individual opportunity and responsibility

Alongside the voluntarist approach, described above, there is a strong message from government exhorting individuals to develop the flexibility and skills they require to make them more employable in an ever-changing labour market. An emphasis on access to educational opportunities is combined with a strong degree of pressure on individuals to take responsibility for their learning and to contribute towards its cost. ILAs, higher education tuition fees for undergraduates and the establishment of the UfI can all be seen as examples of such policies. Within this generic approach towards individual opportunity and responsibility, New Labour has shown itself prepared to target resources and support at vulnerable groups of learners who have traditionally been excluded from the system (eg Educational Maintenance Allowances for some 16–19-year-olds).

Choice and entitlement in the modified market

One very clear theme in New Labour's approach to education and training is its attempt to create a 'modified market' as a half-way point between Conservative marketization and Old Labour regulation and planning. There is a recognition that the quasi-market in education and training has created a system of winners and losers and has not always led to quality or efficiency. Nevertheless, support for a quasi-market is still in evidence in New Labour's stress on a system which is consumer-led rather than provider-led. However, this approach is tempered by funding steers and incentives which are intended to encourage a more equitable distribution of educational opportunities and to promote collaboration and partnership, rather than competition, between providers.

During the Conservative era, a great deal of emphasis was placed on the importance of consumer choice rather than an entitlement to education and training. New Labour, on the other hand, places a greater stress on the latter in terms of access to education and training opportunities. This is the concept which lies behind a 16–19 entitlement curriculum[1] and the Right to Learn legislation for all 16 and 17-year-olds in employment, for example. The problem with the concept of entitlement is that it lies uneasily with New Labour's voluntarist approach because it relies on individuals taking up their entitlement rather than regulation to ensure that the entitlement is provided or exercised. This voluntarist notion of entitlement thus tends to underline the traditional imbalance of power between learner and provider.

New Labour and elites

A final emerging theme is New Labour's apparent reluctance, in the first instance, to tackle elites head-on. Many of the reforms which are currently being pursued in the area of both compulsory and post-compulsory education and training are designed to 'bring up the tail' of underachievers and to tackle social exclusion. However, there appears to be a fear of addressing more fundamental system problems which would require tackling some of the more elite and traditional aspects of the education and training establishment. We have seen that there is a marked reluctance to reform A levels, to threaten fundamentally the position and resourcing of Oxford and Cambridge or to change the funding of sixth forms. The desire to avoid confronting the problem of elitism in the education system could be seen very much as a pragmatic political decision to maintain the commitment of large sections of the middle class to the electoral coalition that brought New Labour to power, and thereby to increase the chance of a second term of office.

These 10 policy themes taken together might be seen as part of a 'weak framework' approach. This is an approach which is characterized by the introduction of initiatives and piecemeal reforms designed to support individual opportunity to participate in education and training, to modify the negative effects of the education and training market and to provide incentives for collaboration, but without putting into place the type of structural reforms required to change the shape of the education and training system as a whole.

As we have seen in earlier chapters of this book, this approach has led both to policy tensions and to a concern that the Government's present policies will not bring about the kind of structural change which is required if the education and training system in this country is to meet the challenges of the 21st century. Chapter 6, for example, illustrates the tensions between New Labour's desire to develop a national qualifications framework which is flexible and inclusive and its desire to preserve A level standards. Chapter 5 poses the question of whether there is a tension between the Government's desire for UK higher education institutions to retain their place in a competitive global market and its goal of widening participation in higher education, while Chapters 2, 3 and 4 all point out the dangers of relying on initiative-led reform and voluntarist measures to make fundamental and necessary changes in the relationship between the labour market and the education and training system in this country. These policy tensions and concerns are now discussed below through the concept of weak and strong framework approaches to policy for the education and training system from 14+.

Weak and strong framework approaches to policy for the education and training system from 14+

Throughout this book we have criticized New Labour for its reliance on voluntarist initiatives which, while practical and focused on the needs of the excluded, may not in the final analysis work effectively because of system barriers. In part, we have argued, this approach has been shaped by New Labour's response to the Conservative legacy. The question we have posed elsewhere and to which we return here is whether, once this legacy has been addressed, New Labour will be prepared to develop its own more distinctive approach, or whether voluntarism is a permanent feature of what has been termed the Third Way.

In order to address this question we will analyse New Labour's overall approach to the education and training system from 14+ through the concept of 'weak' and 'strong' frameworks. We use the term weak framework to describe an approach which places an unrealistic amount of responsibility on individuals to access the type of learning opportunities they require to improve employability and to enter the labour market. This approach attempts to modify the *effects* of the education and training market in three ways. First, within the rubric of personal responsibility outlined above, there is an emphasis on the targeting of limited amounts of state funding to incentivize certain groups of individuals. Second, a weak framework approach also attempts to address divisions within the education and training system by overarching rather than replacing divided structures. Third, there is an attempt to modify the type of institutional competition promoted by the education and training market by creating voluntarist partnerships at local and regional levels. Interestingly, it is also possible to see strong centralized structures (eg DfEE, Ofsted and sectoral funding bodies) as part of a weak framework approach, because they keep power at the centre to regulate market forces, rather than devolving power and resources to regional and local levels to strengthen the type of strong collaborative structures required to assist initiatives or reforms in the longer term. A weak framework approach, therefore, does not alter the structure of the education and training system as a whole, nor does it fundamentally alter the way in which it works.

A strong framework approach, on the other hand, is an attempt to provide structures within the education and training system which support genuine individual empowerment. This involves *modifying the behaviour* of the education and training market by reforming key areas of the education and training system (eg qualifications and funding) to combat long-standing system barriers and divisions. A strong framework approach also provides encouragement for all individuals to participate in education and training by using State funding to provide permanent and balanced incentives for both individuals and institutions. Finally, a strong framework approach requires devolving governmental power in order to strengthen regional and local collaboration to support the individual learner. Examples of strong and weak framework approaches to the education and training system are illustrated in Figure 7.2 (see page 139).

The concept of weak and strong frameworks can be linked to the concept of the Third Way. Like others (eg White, 1998) we have suggested in Chapter 1 of this book that the Third Way is a contested concept of which there are different variants. These variants can differ depending on whether you look at the concept from the perspective of international comparison (eg Hillman, 1998) or, as we do in this chapter, from an historical UK perspective. In the case of international comparison, the Third Way is located 'between the social regulation and inclusivity of continental European social-democratic models and the dynamism and flexible labour markets of North America' (Hillman, 1998: 65). However, from an historical UK perspective, the concept of the Third Way could be seen as lying between Thatcherite free market ideologies and Old Labour state ownership and regulation. If the international comparative location is adopted, then the Third Way approach to education and training policy, in seeking equidistance between European social partnership and US labour market flexibility, will tend to see voluntarism as part of the desired strategy. On the other hand, if the UK historical perspective is adopted to define the parameters of the Third Way in relation to education and training, a voluntarist strategy could be seen simply as a temporary response to the previous Conservative era. In this case, it is possible to see how such a strategy might evolve to embrace a new type of social partnership approach which was not part of the Old Labour paradigm. However, within this position it is also important to recognize that the types of social partnership which exist in countries such as Sweden and Germany are based on strong historic traditions that have never existed in the same way in this country. Direct policy borrowing is, therefore, not an option. We will suggest in the final part of this chapter that the concept of a strong framework provides a way in which the current voluntarist system, which Clough (1999) describes as an 'informal' social partnership model, can be strengthened without mechanically imitating examples from other education and training systems.

Our approach, which connects the concepts of weak and strong frameworks to the Third Way, works principally within the UK historical perspective. We suggest that both weak and strong frameworks lie between the poles of Thatcherite free markets and Old Labour regulation and state ownership and should be viewed as a continuum rather than discrete categories (see Figure 7.1, below). Government policies may, and indeed in New Labour's case do, range across this continuum.

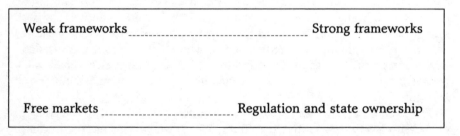

Figure 7.1: *The concept of weak and strong framework approaches to the education and training system from 14+: a continuum*

An example of a weak framework approach can be illustrated through New Labour's Individual Learning Accounts (ILAs) initiative. This represents an element of State intervention in the education and training market aimed at providing purchasing power for particular targeted groups of learners and, thereby, both increasing the number of learners participating in education and training and affecting the type of provision offered by education and training providers. However, there is no compulsion on learners to take up an ILA, nor is there a statutory obligation on employers to contribute to them. The responsibility for taking up an ILA thus rests with the individual in the form of an entitlement. Moreover, until ILAs represent significant resources for education and training providers they are unlikely to have a major effect on their behaviour. ILAs can, therefore, be regarded as part of a weak framework approach because they are a voluntarist, small-scale and isolated initiative which is not backed up by more fundamental system change.

A strong framework approach to ILAs, on the other hand, would be signalled by a larger injection of funds, obligations on employers to support the individual taking up the ILA and the establishment of a 'Learning Bank' to support joint investment in education and training. The regulatory aspect of this approach is not an attempt to emphasize the power of the provider over that of the learner. The process of regulation would be designed to empower individuals by placing obligations on others to resource and support them in their choices.

Further features of weak and strong frameworks can be illustrated through a comparison of five dimensions of policy related to education and training from 14+ (see Figure 7.2, below).

Policy dimensions	A weak framework approach	A strong framework approach
Employers and work-based learning	• voluntary employer training organizations (eg NTOs); • voluntary approach within national guidelines for NT and MA programmes; • individual entitlement to training (eg Right to Learn legislation for 16–17-year-olds).	• stronger social partnership arrangements between government, employers and trade unions; • modified levy and taxation policy for training in the workplace; • licence to trade; • employer statutory obligation to train; • strengthened national framework for NT and MA programmes in all sectors.
Funding for education and training	• small-scale incentives for individuals (eg ILAs and Career Development Loans); • unco-ordinated funding steers for different sectors.	• co-ordinated approach to individual funding (eg Learning Bank); • unified post-16 institutional funding system.

Learning opportunities	• Initiatives designed to promote individual access to learning (eg Ufl, ILAs and Learning Direct); • Incentives and sanctions framework in relation to welfare and benefits (eg New Deal and Educational Maintenance Allowances).	• a local and regional network of access, guidance and progression routes underpinned by a unified national qualifications framework; • co-ordinated approach to benefits, education and employment.
Qualifications and curriculum	• Divided, non-inclusive national qualifications framework with limited linkages.	• a single, unified and inclusive qualifications system from 14+ with credit accumulation and transfer.
Organization, delivery and co-ordination	• competing local institutions (sixth forms, colleges and HEIs); • weak local partnership bodies (eg LEAs and TECs/CCTEs); • voluntary strategic bodies (eg NTOs); • sector-specific quality assurance agencies (eg Ofsted, FEFC, QAA) dominated by top-down and accountability approaches; • strong centralized government organizations (eg DfEE, regulatory and awarding bodies); • weak regional bodies (eg RDAs); • initiative-led cross-departmental collaboration (eg SEU); • national targets as a focus for voluntary action.	• local tertiary systems including schools, colleges, HEIs and workplaces; • harmonized quality assurance systems designed for more bottom-up and self-improvement oriented approaches; • national government organizations working alongside a strong regional framework; • regional framework of partnership and planning supported by stronger social partnership arrangements, funding and legislation; • national targets as a focus for strategic planning.

Figure 7.2: *A comparison of weak and strong framework approaches to policy for the 14+ education and training system*

Below we briefly elaborate on the different policy dimensions outlined in Figure 7.2 in relation to the concept of weak and strong frameworks. We then attempt to situate New Labour within this and to highlight where policies already indicate movement along the weak/strong continuum. We do, however, recognize the danger of polarizing positions through the use of a matrix of this type. It is important to stress here that some of the initiatives which we currently locate within the weak framework approach, such as UfI, would undoubtedly work better within the type of strong framework approach that we describe in this chapter. Similarly there are structures, such as RDAs, which we have associated with a weak framework approach, simply because their current form is ill-defined rather than because they inherently belong in this category. There is no reason why RDAs should not eventually evolve into the type of strong regional framework of partnership and planning which we see as an essential aspect of a strong framework approach (see, for example, Pearce and Hillman, 1998).

Employers and work-based learning

As described in Chapter 4, a weak framework approach to the labour market and training would be characterized by a voluntarist approach to employers, national guidelines for work-based training programmes and an individual entitlement to training, but with no compulsion on different sectors of the labour market to develop training programmes or to provide training for individual employees. A strong framework approach, on the other hand, would involve new types of social partnership arrangements between government, employers and trade unions (Clough, 1999) to underpin policies such as a national framework of high quality National Traineeships and Modern Apprenticeships in all sectors; a modified levy and taxation policy for training in the workplace with a statutory obligation for employers to provide or pay for an agreed amount of training; and regulation around licence to trade. The latter approach would be designed to stimulate employer demand for skills, particularly in small and medium-sized enterprises.

Currently the majority of New Labour's policies in this area lie at the weak framework end of the continuum because of their reliance on a voluntary approach and their desire not to make more demands on employers over and above that of current social legislation such as that outlined in the *Fairness at Work* (DTI, 1998b). However, their support for training partnerships and initiatives which involve trade unions as well as employers (eg The Union Learning Fund) might be seen as a small move in the direction towards the development of a stronger framework for training in the workplace.

Funding for education and training

A weak framework approach to funding for education and training attempts to modify the effects of the market through funding steers in different sectors. However, these do not shape the system as a whole, nor do they significantly alter the competitive relationship between institutions. In addition, a weak framework approach to funding involves incentivizing specific targeted groups of learners to participate in education and training. New Labour's targeted widening participation funding for the further and higher education sectors could be seen as part of this weak framework approach. So, too, could initiatives such as ILAs and Career Development Loans. A move towards a strong framework approach in this area would mean developing a more co-ordinated system of funding for all learners through, for example, the setting up of a Learning Bank and a more unified and common methodology for funding all post-16 providers. As earlier chapters of this book have stated, New Labour has indicated a willingness to examine the latter approach, but there is no strong move in this direction at present.

Learning opportunities

In terms of creating and supporting learning opportunities, a weak framework approach would consist of developing a series of initiatives designed to promote individual learner access. The UfI, ILAs and Learning Direct provide good examples of New Labour's weak framework approach in this area. The development of a local and regional network of transparent access, guidance and progression routes, underpinned by a unified national qualifications framework with credit accumulation and transfer possibilities, on the other hand, would characterize a strong framework approach in this area. It would also ensure that initiatives, such as UfI and ILAs, were themselves able to work more effectively. Chapters 2 and 6 indicate that New Labour still has some way to go in developing this type of network.

In addition, it would also be necessary to underpin a strong framework for learning by a co-ordinated approach to benefit, education and employment incentives and sanctions which would affect all sections of the population rather than specifically targeted groups (see Chapter 3). There is some indication that New Labour would like to move in this direction, but it has already experienced problems with developing a more integrated approach to welfare and benefit reform.

Qualifications and curriculum

In the area of qualifications reform, as Chapter 6 points out, New Labour is following a classic example of a weak framework approach represented by the development of a limited range of linkages within a divided and incomplete national qualifications system.[2] A strong framework approach, on the other hand, would involve the building of a single, unified and inclusive qualifications system from 14+ with credit accumulation and transfer possibilities. New Labour is currently still firmly at the weak framework end of the continuum and appears to have considerable reservations about moving to a strong framework approach, at least in the short term.

Organization, delivery and co-ordination

A final broad dimension of policy for education and training from 14+ which lends itself to categorization into weak and strong framework approaches is the area of organization, delivery and co-ordination. Here a weak framework approach might be used to describe New Labour's current centralist but 'modified market' and voluntarist approach to this area. What this translates into is a mix of strong central government organizations (eg DfEE, QCA) with national targets as a focus for voluntary action, initiative-led cross-departmental collaboration (eg the work of the SEU), voluntary strategic and regional bodies (eg NTOs and RDAs), weak local partnerships and agencies (eg LEAs, TECs, CCTEs) and competing local institutions (eg sixth forms, further education colleges and higher education institutions). This might be compared with a strong framework approach in this area which would involve the creation of local tertiary systems, a responsive and well-resourced structure for regional partnership and planning (supported by the type of new social partnership arrangements described earlier in this section), led by strong national government organizations with planned cross-departmental collaboration and national targets as a focus for strategic planning.

In summary, by rejecting both market-led and regulatory approaches to the education and training system from 14+, New Labour has arguably opted for a weak framework approach to policy in this area. This is a strategy in which the market still heavily influences the actions of institutions and individuals, but which is being gradually modified through a framework of government-sponsored initiatives, financial incentives and various forms of voluntary partnership at local, regional and national level.

Towards a strong framework approach: an agenda for a second Parliament

We argue that this weak framework approach to the education and training system from 14+ will be inadequate to tackle a number of key challenges which threaten to prevent New Labour achieving its current and future aims in this area. Moreover, we suggest that New Labour may be forced to move towards a strong framework approach to deliver its declared goals in a second term of office. Below, we briefly describe four system challenges – the need to address the low skills equilibrium through the development of new social partnerships; the need for structural change to overcome system barriers and to build an infrastructure for lifelong learning; the need for an all-through qualifications system to lever up levels of participation, achievement and progression and to move beyond system stasis; and the need to decide on the direction of development for the education and training system as a whole. In each case, we suggest what a move towards a strong framework approach might involve.

The role of social partnership in addressing the low skills equilibrium

Despite rises in full-time participation in post-compulsory education and training, there is plenty of evidence of the persistence of the low skills equilibrium originally identified by Finegold and Soskise (1988) and described in Chapter 4. Weak frameworks do not address this problem because they do not challenge traditional employer attitudes and behaviour towards education, training and qualifications.

We argued above that there is a need for a new type of social partnership approach in this country which makes more concerted demands of employers, as is the case in some other European countries (Green, 1997). The Bargaining for Skills initiatives and the Rt Hon David Blunkett's encouragement of trade unions to play an active part in promoting and supporting lifelong learning are only the first steps in this direction. These initiatives will have to be underpinned by a degree of compulsion, such as a modified levy system or an obligation on employers to train, in order to empower learners and to create a culture in which employers are encouraged to invest in training rather than to poach. This would go some way to ensure that the practices of the best employers, rather than the worst, become the basis of partnership and collaboration in this area.

Devolved structures and funding frameworks to underpin lifelong learning

In Chapters 2, 3, 4 and 5, which are concerned with various aspects of lifelong learning, we point out the dangers of relying on initiatives-led reform and voluntarist measures which underestimate the support individuals will require not only to access learning but also to progress and achieve. We argue in these chapters for the need to replace the current marketized education and training system by devolved local and regional structures to support a collaborative framework of providers, funding systems and an all-through qualifications system to support lifelong learning. It is possible to see the RDAs as an important step in this direction, but these organizations will have to be reinforced by the kind of new social partnership arrangements described above, by strong funding levers and by radical but staged qualifications reform.

Developing an all-through qualifications framework

While qualifications reform is central to tackling all the challenges outlined above, it also has a special role to play in levering up levels of participation, achievement and progression. In Chapter 6, we have described an education and training system inherited from the Conservatives which is no longer experiencing strong rises in participation and attainment levels. New Labour has responded by putting into place strong measures in compulsory education (eg a national numeracy and literacy strategy), but has shown a reluctance to address one of the major system barriers for both compulsory and post-compulsory education – the current exclusive 14+ qualifications arrangements dominated by the culture and methods of the academic/general track. We argue that a key feature of a strong framework approach to the education and training system from 14+ is the development of an inclusive, flexible and progressive qualifications and curriculum system which sees as its prime objective raising levels of achievement and supporting knowledge and skills for the 21st century.

Overall direction for the education and training system from 14+

As Chapter 5 points out, New Labour's inheritance was an education and training system that had, over the previous decade, 'drifted' into a weak education-based and mass marketized further and higher education model. We have argued that, as a result of marketization, the different education sectors (eg school sixth forms, further education colleges and higher institutions) have tended to compete rather than to collaborate over the provision of lifelong learning opportunities. This has resulted in a number of distortions, for example, duplication of provision, funding inefficiencies, poor quality programmes and low status institutions, all of which have worked against the interests of learners. Moreover, the role that work-based learning has played in either the education of young people or the continuing education and training of older learners has been haphazard. Consequently, this type of education and training has often been regarded as low level and second-rate.

What New Labour is doing is modifying this marketized system by making it more inclusive at both the lower (basic skills and further education) and the higher levels (higher education). However, the Government does not appear to be able to respond clearly to calls for a more European-oriented social partnership model, which seeks to develop quality vocational education and training and strong local and regional partnerships, because of the regulatory implications this would require. The result is that beyond the strategies of social inclusion and raising the basic skills of the workforce, New Labour does not appear to know what kind of direction it wishes the education and training system to follow.

We have argued that the current weak education-based model described above should be reinforced by a work-based route which has strong relationships with further and higher education. This needs to be underpinned by the type of new social partnership framework, regional collaboration and the all-through qualifications system described above which, among other things, aim to improve the quality and status of vocational learning at Level 3 and above. Throughout this book, we have argued that much of the education and training system expansion and shape have been the result of marketization and a weak employer contribution. We would suggest that both these factors need to be addressed through the strong framework approach we have described in this chapter in order to shape the type of education and training system this country needs for the new millennium.

Final comments

Throughout this book we have looked at New Labour's policies before and after the general election. We have argued that the realities of government have, not surprisingly, introduced increased caution and compromise. While being in government is far more difficult than ever envisaged in opposition (and New Labour prepared more than most for this eventuality), we believe that the best way to tackle difficult decisions and political processes is to be clear about future direction.

Our principle criticism of New Labour's current Third Way approach to the post-14 education and training system is that it avoids giving a clear picture of where the system is heading and how current policies will contribute to a move in this direction. This analysis suggests that the picture painted by Showstack-Sassoon (1998), of a Labour Government inching its way forward and, in the process, gradually creating more ideological space, could be self-defeating. Earlier in this chapter, we have suggested that New Labour's 'covert evolutionary' style of reform deliberately avoids creating ideological space because of its reluctance to engage in open debate and its desire to stick instead to the pursuit of a policy hierarchy and voluntarist policy measures.

Those in education will try to understand the difficulties faced by a new government tackling the problems left by the legacy of the previous administration and its consequent focus on initiatives which can be achieved within one term of office. New Labour has been forced to devote its efforts to remediation. Moreover, there is a great deal of sympathy and support for this Government's desire to pursue the agendas of widening participation and addressing social and educational exclusion. This is both a laudable aim and long overdue.

However, we have suggested that New Labour's current concept of the Third Way in post-14 education and training, marked by a pervasive voluntarism, does not provide an adequate agenda for future change. We have argued the need for the current Third Way strategies, which have been described as part of a weak framework approach, to be superseded by another Third Way strategy which we have termed a strong framework approach.

We therefore suggest that the move towards a strong framework approach should begin now, not after 2001, and should be part of the build-up to a new manifesto for a second Parliament. For a party that has never achieved a second term in office, clearly the first objective is to be re-elected. However, New Labour will not be remembered for having been re-elected, but for the permanent changes it brought about in government. In our area, this means altering the shape, structure and behaviour of the education and training system and this process has hardly begun.

Notes

1 The term 'entitlement curriculum' in relation to 16–19-year-olds in further education colleges is used in the Government's response to the House of Commons Education and Employment Select Committee Report on further education (House of Commons, 1999).
2 The concept of weak and strong frameworks was originally developed in relation to the Dearing Review of qualifications (Spours and Young, 1996).

References

Ainley, P and Corney, M (1990) *Training for the Future: The rise and fall of the Manpower Services Commission*, Cassell, London

Association for Colleges (AfC), The Girls' School Association (GSA), The Headmasters' Conference (HMC), The Secondary Heads' Association (SHA), The Sixth Form Colleges' Association (APVIC) and The Society for Headmasters and Headmistresses in Independent Schools (SHMIS) (1994) *Post-compulsory Education and Training: A joint statement*, AfC, London

Association of Colleges (1998) *Briefing on the New Deal*, AoC, London, May

Association of Colleges and Further Education Development Agency (1998) *New Deal: Over-25 initiative*, AoC, London

Avis, J et al (1996) *Knowledge and Nationhood: Education, politics and work*, Cassell, London

Barnett, R (1994) *The Limits of Competence: Knowledge, higher education and society*, SRHE/Open University Press, Buckingham

Bates, I et al (1984) *Schooling for the Dole?*, Macmillan, London

Beales, R (1998) Meeting New Deal student support needs, *FEDA Conference: A New Deal in Practice*, November

Beattie, A (1997) *Working People and Lifelong Learning: A study of the impact of an employee development scheme*, NIACE, Leicester

Beaumont, G (1995) *Review of 100 NVQs and SVQs: A report submitted to the DfEE*, DfEE, London

Beverley, L (1998) *The New Deal: Issues for colleges*, London Regional Post-16 Network, Post-16 Education Centre, Institute of Education, University of London

Bivand, P (1998) Sudden jump in education and training option, *Working Brief No 100*, Unemployment Unit, London

Blackstone, Baroness (1998) *New National Learning Targets for 2002*, Letter from the DfEE, 28 October

Blair, Rt Hon T (1996) *New Britain: My vision of a young country*, Fourth Estate, London

Blair, Rt Hon T (1997) Speech by the Prime Minister, the Right Honourable Tony Blair, MP, at the Aylesbury Estate, Southwark, 2 June

Blair, Rt Hon T (1999) *Speech on the Occasion of the 10th Anniversary of the Institute for Public Policy Research*, 10 Downing Street Press Office, London

Blunkett, Rt Hon D (1997) New Deal for the Unemployed, *New Labour: New Britain*, Summer

Brown, Rt Hon G (1994) *University for Industry: Turning the workplace into a centre of continuous learning*, Labour Party, London

Brown, Rt Hon G (1996) *Equality of Opportunity and the Welfare State,* community care lecture, 22 October

References

Brown, Rt Hon G, Blunkett, Rt Hon D and Harman, Rt Hon H (1996) *Equipping Young People for the Future: From welfare to education*, A Report from Labour's Review of the Financing of Post-16 Education, Labour Party, London

Bynner, J and Parsons, S (1997) *It Doesn't Get Any Better: The impact of poor basic skills on the lives of 37-year-olds*, Basic Skills Agency (BSA), London

Callaghan, Rt Hon J (1976) Ruskin College Speech, *The Times Educational Supplement*, 22 October

Capey, J (1996) *Review of GNVQ Assessment*, National Council for Vocational Qualifications, London

Case, C and Atkins, S (1998) *Focus on the New Deal: Expectations and understanding based on previous experience of training and the Job Seeker's Allowance*, Sheffield Youth Service and the Youth Association of South Yorkshire

Clough, B (1998) Saving to learn, *'t' magazine – training, education and employment*, Dec–Jan 1998–99

Clough, B (1999 forthcoming) *Social Partnership: Added value or added burden? VET systems in the UK and Germany*, High Skills Project Working Paper, Institute of Education, University of London

Cockett, M and Callaghan, J (1996) Caught in the middle – transition at 16+, in *Education and Training: Chaos or coherence*, ed R Halsall and M Cockett, David Fulton Publications, London

Coffield, F (1997) *Can the UK Become a Learning Society?*, The 4th Annual Education Lecture, RSA

Coffield, F and Vignoles, A (1997) Widening participation in higher education by ethnic minorities, women and alternative students, in National Committee of Inquiry into Higher Education, *Higher Education in the Learning Society*, NCIHE, London

Coffield, F and Williamson, B (1997) *Repositioning Higher Education*, SRHE and Open University Press, Buckingham

Commission on Social Justice/Institute for Public Policy Research (1994) *Strategies for National Renewal*, Vintage, London

Confederation of British Industry (1989) *Towards a Skills Revolution: Report of the vocational education and training task force*, CBI, London

Confederation of British Industry (1993) *Routes for Success*, CBI, London

Convery, P (1998) New turbulence in the claimant count, *Working Brief No 90*, Unemployment Unit, London

Corrie, D (1997) Macroeconomic policy and stakeholder capitalism, in *Stakeholder Capitalism*, ed G Kelly, D Kelly and A Gamble, Macmillan, London

Crequer, N (1998) Strings on Blunkett's bonus, *Times Educational Supplement*, p18, December

Crosland, A (1965) Speech at Woolwich Polytechnic, 27 April

Dearing, Sir Ron (1996) *Review of Qualifications for 16–19-year-olds*, SCAA, London

Department for Education (DfE) (1992) *The Further and Higher Education Act*, HMSO, London

Department for Education (DfE) (1995) *Lifetime Learning: A consultation document*, Crown Copyright, London

Department for Education/Employment Department/Welsh Office (DfE/ED/WO) (1991) *Education and Training for the 21st Century*, HMSO, London

Department for Education and Employment (DfEE) (1996) *Lifetime Learning: A policy framework*, Crown Copyright, London

DfEE (1997a) *Qualifying for Success: A consultation paper on the future of post-16 qualifications*, DfEE, London
DfEE (1997b) *Excellence in Schools*, The Stationery Office, London
DfEE (1997c) *Education and Training Development Agenda 1997–98*, DfEE, London
DfEE (1997d) *National Training Organizations Prospectus 1998–99*, DfEE, London
DfEE (1997e) Government defers A level and GNVQ reform, Press Notice, 11 June, DfEE, London
DfEE (1997f) *Building the Framework: A consultation paper on bringing together the work of the National Council for Vocational Qualifications and the School Curriculum and Assessment Authority*, DfEE, London
DfEE (1997g) *Guaranteeing Standards: A consultation paper on the structure of awarding bodies*, DfEE, London
DfEE (1997h) *Investing in Young People: A strategy for the education and training of 16–18-year-olds*, Crown Copyright, London
DfEE (1998a) *The Learning Age: A renaissance for a New Britain*, DfEE, London
DfEE (1998b) *Higher Education for the 21st Century: Response to the Dearing Report*, DfEE, London
DfEE (1998c) *Local Information, Advice and Guidance for Adults in England – Towards a national framework*, Crown Copyright, Sheffield
DfEE (1998d) *University for Industry: Engaging people in learning for life*, Pathfinder Prospectus, DfEE, London
DfEE (1998e) New Deal for the long-term unemployed takes cynics by surprise, Howarth press statement 298/98, DfEE, London
DfEE (1998f) *Qualifying for Success: The response to the Qualifications and Curriculum Authority's advice*, Letter from Baroness Tessa Blackstone to Sir William Stubbs, 3 April
DfEE (1998g) *25 plus: Design of New Deal pilots*, DfEE, London
DfEE (1998h) *New Deal for Long-term Unemployed People Aged 25 Plus*, DfEE, London
DfEE (1998i) *New Deal for Young People: Statistics bulletin 322/98*, DfEE, London
DfEE (1998j) Big firms sign up to the New Deal, *Employment News No 260*, DfEE, Sheffield
DfEE (1998k) *Towards a National Skills Agenda: First report of the National Skills Task Force*, DfEE, London
DfEE (1998l) *Learning and Working Together for the Future: A strategic framework to 2002*, Crown Copyright, London
DfEE (1998m) *A Proposed 'Gateway' to Learning for the Most Disadvantaged 16 and 17-year-olds*, DfEE, London
DfEE (1998n) *United Kingdom Employment Action Plan*, DfEE, London
DfEE (1998o) *Further Education for the New Millennium: Response to the Kennedy Report*, DfEE, London
DfEE (1998p) *Further Education Funding for 1999-2001*, Letter from R J Dawe to Professor David Melville, 8 December
DfEE (1998q) *New Arrangements for Effective Student Support in Further Education*, Report of the Further Education Student Support Group, DfEE, London
DfEE (1998r) *Accountability in Further Education: A consultation paper*, DfEE, London
DfEE (1998s) Blackstone sets out proposals to boost FE accountability and partnerships, DfEE Press Release 113/98, 5 March

References

DfEE (1999a) *Lifelong Learning Partnerships*, Letter from Rt Hon David Blunkett to Chief Education Officers, College Principals, TEC Chief Executives, Careers Service Chief Executives, 4 January

DfEE (1999b) *Lifelong Learning Partnerships Remit*, DfEE, London

DfEE (1999c) *The Introduction of the New Key Skills Qualification and Revised GNVQ*, Letter from Baroness Tessa Blackstone to Sir William Stubbs, 22 January

DfEE, Training and Employment Agency, Department of Education Northern Ireland, The Scottish Office and The Welsh Office (1998) *University for Industry: Pathfinder prospectus*, Crown Copyright, London

Department of Education and Science (1988) *The Education Reform Act*, HMSO, London

Department of Social Security (DSS) (1997) *Welfare Reform Focus Files*, Central Office of Information, London

Department of the Environment, Transport and the Regions (DETR) (1997) *Building Partnerships for Prosperity*, DETR, London

DETR (1998) *Regional Development Agencies: Draft guidance on RDAs' strategies*, DETR, London

Department of Trade and Industry (DTI) (1994) *Competitiveness: Helping business win*, HMSO, London

DTI (1995) *Competitiveness: Forging ahead*, HMSO, London

DTI (1998a) *Competitiveness UK: Our partnership with business*, DTI, London

DTI (1998b) *Fairness at Work White Paper*, DTI, London

Donnelly, C (1997a) Capping education levels for the young unemployed, *Working Brief No 89*, Unemployment Unit, London

Donnelly, C (1997b) Benefits sanctions do not deter rule-breaking, *Working Brief No 89*, Unemployment Unit, London

Educa (1998) New Deal, *Educa*, **183**, Guildford Education Services

Education and Employment Committee (1998) *Further Education*, The Stationery Office, London

Elliott, L (1998) Forget the unthinkable, remember the economy, the *Guardian*, 10 August

Employment Service (1998a) *What is the New Deal for Young People?* Employment Service, Sheffield

Employment Service (1998b) *25+ Planning Guidance*, Employment Service, Sheffield

Evans, K *et al* (1997) Working to Learn: A work-based route to learning for young people, *Issues in People Management*, **18**, Institute of Personnel and Development

FEDA/Institute of Education/Nuffield Foundation (1997) *GNVQs 1993–97: A national survey report*, FEDA, London

Finegold, D (1993) The emerging post-16 system: analysis and critique, in *The Reform of Post-16 Education and Training in England and Wales*, ed W Richardson, J Woolhouse and D Finegold, Longman, Harlow

Finegold, D and Soskise, D (1988) The failure of training in Britain: analysis and prescription, *Oxford Review of Economic Policy*, **4** (3), Oxford University Press, Oxford

Finegold, D *et al* (1990) *A British Baccalaureate: Overcoming division between education and training*, Institute for Public Policy Research, London

Finn, D (1997) Labour's New Deal for the Unemployed: making it work locally, *Local Economy*, November

Finn, D (1998) Labour's New Deal for the Unemployed and the stricter benefit regime, *Social Policy Review*, **10**

Foyer Federation (1998) *Opening Doors for Young People*, Foyer Federation, London

Fryer, R (1997) *Learning for the 21st Century: First report of the National Advisory Group for Continuing Education and Lifelong Learning*, NAGfCELL, London

Further Education Funding Council (1997) *How to Widen Participation: A guide to good practice*, FEFC, Coventry

Gibbons, M (1996) Massification of higher education and the organization of research, in *Higher Education and Lifelong Learning*, ed F Coffield, Department of Education, University of Newcastle upon Tyne

Giddens, A (1994) *Beyond Left and Right: The future of radical politics*, Polity Press, Cambridge

Giddens, A (1998) *The Third Way: The renewal of social democracy*, Polity Press, Cambridge

Gray, J, Jesson, D and Tranmer, M (1993) *Boosting Post-16 Participation in Full-time Education: A study of some key factors in England and Wales*, Youth Cohort Study No 20, Sheffield Employment Department

Green, A (1997) *Education, Globalization and the Nation State*, Macmillan Press, Basingstoke

Green, A and Lucas, N, eds (1999) *FE and Lifelong Learning: Realigning the sector for the 21st century*, IOE, London

Green, F and Francis, D (1992) Skill shortages and skill deficiency: a critique, *Work, Employment and Society*, **6**, pp 287–301

Green, G (1998) *Four Failures of the New Deal*, Centre for Policy Studies, London

Hargreaves, A (1989) *Curriculum and Assessment Reform*, Open University Press, Buckingham

Hasluck, C *et al* (1997) *Modern Apprenticeships: A survey of employers*, DfEE Research Studies, RS **53**, Crown Copyright, London

Hatcher, R (1994) Labour's Green Paper: The limits of consensus, *Forum 36*, **3**, pp 91–92

Hatcher, R (1998) Labour, official school improvement and equality, *Journal of Education Policy*, **13** (4), pp 485–99

Higher Education Funding Council for England (1998) *Widening Participation in Higher Education: Funding proposals*, HEFCE, Bristol

Hillman, J (1996) *University for Industry: Creating a national learning network*, IPPR, London

Hillman, J (1998) The Labour Government and lifelong learning, *Renewal*, **6** (2), pp 63–72, Spring

Hirst, P and Thompson, G (1996) *Globalization in Question: The international economy and possibilities of governance*, Polity Press, Cambridge

Hodgson, A (1999) Analysing education and training policies for tackling social exclusion, in *Tackling Disaffection and Social Exclusion*, ed A Hayton, Kogan Page, London

Hodgson, A and Kambouri, M (1999) Adults as lifelong learners: the role of pedagogy in the new policy context, in *Pedagogy and its Impact on Learning*, ed P Mortimer, Sage, London

Hodgson, A and Spours, K (1997a) From the 1991 White Paper to the Dearing Report: a conceptual and historical framework for the 1990s, in *Dearing and Beyond: 14–19 qualifications, frameworks and systems*, ed A Hodgson and K Spours, Kogan Page, London

References

Hodgson, A and Spours, K, eds (1997b) *Dearing and Beyond: 14–19 qualifications, frameworks and systems*, Kogan Page, London

Hodgson, A and Spours, K (1998) Pushed too far?, *Times Educational Supplement*, 11 December

Hodgson, A, Spours, K and Young, M (1998) Broader and broader still in post-16 education, *Times Educational Supplement*, 16 May

Hodkinson, P and Sparkes A (1994) The myth of the market: the negotiation of training in a Youth Credits Pilot Scheme, *British Journal of Education and Work*, **7** (3)

House of Commons (1999) *Government Response to the Sixth Report from the Education and Employment Committee, Session 1997–98*, The Stationery Office, London

Howieson, C *et al* (1997) Unifying academic and vocational learning: the state of the debate in England and Scotland, *Journal of Education and Work*, **10** (1)

Hutton, W (1995) *The State We're In*, Jonathon Cape, London

Institute of Education (IOE) (1997) *DfEE Consultation Paper on the Future of Post-16 Qualifications: Qualifying for success – a response*, Institute of Education, University of London

Jenkins, C and David, J (1996) *The Welsh Baccalaureate*, Institute of Welsh Affairs, Cardiff

Joint Associations Curriculum Group (1997) *The Next Step Towards a New Curriculum Framework Post-16*, JACG, Wigan

Jupp, T and Scribbens, J (1998) *New Deal: Note to inner London principals*, South Thames College, London

Keep, E and Mayhew, K (1996a) Towards a learning society – definition and measurement, *Policy Studies*, **17** (3), pp 215–32

Keep, E and Mayhew, K (1996b) Evaluating assumptions that underlie training policy, in *Acquiring Skills: Market failures, their symptoms and policy responses*, ed A Booth and D Snower, Cambridge University Press, Cambridge

Keep, E and Mayhew, K (1997) Vocational education and training and economic performance, in *Britain's Economic Performance*, ed T Buxton, T Chapman and P Temple, Routledge, London

Kennedy, H (1997) *Learning Works: Widening participation in further education*, FEFC, Coventry

Kypri, P (1998) *The New Deal and FE*, FEDA, London

Labour Party (1973) *Higher and Further Education Report of Labour Party Study Group*, Labour Party, London

Labour Party (1986) *Education and Training: Options for Labour*, Labour Party, London

Labour Party (1991) *Quality Assured: A consultative document outlining Labour's proposals for safeguarding and enhancing standards in higher education*, Labour Party, London

Labour Party (1992a) *Opening Doors*, Labour Party, London

Labour Party (1992b) *The Open University: The key to wider opportunities*, Labour Party, London

Labour Party (1994) *University for Industry*, Labour Party, London

Labour Party (1995a) *A New Economic Future for Britain: Economic and employment opportunities for all*, 1995 conference, Labour Party, London

Labour Party (1995b) *Labour's New Deal for Britain's Under-25s*, Labour Party, London

Labour Party (1996a) *Lifelong Learning*, Labour Party, London

Labour Party (1996b) *Aiming Higher: Labour's proposals for the reform of the 14–19 curriculum*, Labour Party, London

Labour Party (1996c) *Equipping Young People for the Future: From welfare to education: A report from Labour's review of financing post-16 education*, Labour Party, London

Labour Party (1996d) *Learn as You Earn: Labour's plans for a skills revolution*, Labour Party, London

Labour Party (1996e) *Getting Welfare to Work*, Labour Party, London

Labour Party (1996f) *New Deal for a Lost Generation*, Labour Party, London

Labour Party (1997) *Labour Party General Election Manifesto 1997: Because Britain deserves better*, Labour Party, London

Lasonen, J and Young, M, eds (1998) *Strategies for Achieving Parity of Esteem in European Upper Secondary Education*, Institute for Educational Research, University of Jyvaskyla, Finland

Layard, R (1995) *Preventing Long-term Unemployment*, Employment Policy Institute, London

Liberal Democrats (1993) *Excellence for All: Fourteen plus*, Liberal Democrats, London

London TEC Council (1997) *Making the New Deal Work in London*, London TEC Council, London

McCaig, C (1997) *Labour's Policy Development in Opposition: Constraints on action*, Draft chapter of doctorate thesis, University of Sheffield

McCarthy, W (1997) *New Labour at Work: Reforming the labour market*, Institute of Public Policy Research, London

McNair, S (1998) *The Invisible Majority – Adult Learners in English Higher Education*, Paper given at Socrates HE Project Seminar, 24 April

Macrae, S, Maguire, M and Ball, S (1997) Whose 'learning society'?, A tentative deconstruction, *Journal of Education Policy*, **12** (6), pp 499–509

Maguire, M (1998) Modern Apprenticeships and employers, *Journal of Vocational Education and Training*, **50** (2), pp 247–58

Miliband, D (1991) *Learning by Right: An entitlement to paid education and training*, IPPR, London

Miliband, D, ed (1994) *Reinventing the Left*, IPPR/Polity Press, London

Milner, H, Hillman, J, Pearce, N, and Thorne, M (1999) *Piloting the University for Industry: Report of the north-east project*, IPPR, London

Mulgan, G (1998) Social exclusion: joined-up solutions to joined-up problems, in *An Inclusive Society: Strategies for tackling poverty*, ed C Oppenheim, IPPR, London

Murray, R (1991) The State after Henry, *Marxism Today*, pp 22–27, May

Nash, I and Nicholls, A (1997) 'Dearth of expertise' in Open Learning, *Times Educational Supplement*, 11 July

National Advisory Council for Education and Training Targets (NACETT) (1998) *Fast Forward for Skills: A summary of NACETT's report on the future of National Targets for Education and Training*, NACETT, London

National Association of Headteachers (1995) *Proposals on 14–19 Education*, NAHT, Haywards Heath

National Commission on Education (1993) Learning to Succeed: A radical look at education today and a strategy for the future, *Report of the Paul Hamlyn Foundation*, Heinemann, Oxford

National Commission on Education (1995) Learning to Succeed: The way ahead, *Report of the Paul Hamlyn Foundation*, National Commission on Education, London

References

National Committee of Inquiry into Higher Education (NCIHE) (1997) *Higher Education in the Learning Society Summary Report*, NCIHE, London

Nigel Blagg Associates (1998) *New Deal Client Survey*, Nigel Blagg Associates, Taunton

Nimmo, M (1997) Welfare to Work and incentives to work, *Working Brief No 89*, Unemployment Unit, London

Office of National Statistics (1997) *Adult Literacy in Britain*, The Stationery Office, London

Oppenheim, C (1998) Poverty and social exclusion: an overview, in *An Inclusive Society: Strategies for tackling poverty*, ed C Oppenheim, IPPR, London

Organisation for Economic Co-operation and Development (OECD) (1996) *Lifelong Learning for All*, OECD, Paris

Organisation for Economic Co-operation and Development (OECD) (1998) *Synthesis of Country Reports on Alternative Approaches to Financing Lifelong Learning*, OECD, Paris

Payne, J (1998) The attractions of joined-up thinking, *Adults Learning*, **10** (4)

Pearce, N and Hillman, J (1998) *Wasted Youth: Raising achievement and tackling social exclusion*, Institute of Public Policy Research, London

Perraton, J (1997) The global economy, in *Stakeholder Capitalism*, ed J Perraton, Macmillan, London

Plant, R (1998) *The Third Way*, Working Paper, Friedrich Ebert Stiftung/Europe Policy Forum Seminar, 20 July, Friedrich Ebert Stiftung

Qualifications and Curriculum Authority (QCA) (1998a) *1998 A level, GCSE and Part 1 results*, G and GVQ Committee 17/98, QCA, London

QCA (1998b) *Evaluation of the first year of the Key Skills Pilot: Note to officials*, QCA internal document

QCA (1999) Flexibility for adult learners within the national qualifications framework and Improving the value of NVQs and other vocational qualifications, Two papers produced as part of the consultation on flexibility within the National Qualifications Framework, QCA, London

QCA/CCEA/ACCAC (1998) *An Overarching Certificate at Advanced Level: Research specification*, QCA, London

Raffe, D (1992) Beyond the 'Mixed Model', in *Social Research and Social Reform*, ed C Crouch and A Heath, Clarendon Press, Oxford

Raffe, D *et al* (1997) *The Unification of Post-compulsory Education: Towards a conceptual framework*, Unified Learning Project Working Paper 2, Post 16 Education Centre, Institute of Education and Centre for Educational Sociology, University of Edinburgh

Rafferty, F (1998) Small Sixth Forms Cost Country £500m, *Times Educational Supplement*, 16 October

Rees, G (1997) Vocational education and training and regional development: an analytical framework, *Journal of Education and Work*, **10** (2), pp 141-49

Reich, R (1991) *The Work of Nations*, Simon and Schuster, New York

Reisenberger, A and Sanders, J (1997) *Adult Learners: Pathways to progression*, FEDA, Blagdon

Richardson, W (1998) Work-based learning for young people: national policy, 1994–1997, *Journal of Vocational Education and Training*, **50** (2), pp 225–46

Richardson, W and Gumbley, N (1995) *Foundation Learning in the Work-based Route*, Learning for the Future, Working Paper No 4, University of Warwick and Institute of Education, University of London

Richardson *et al* (1995) *Learning for the Future: Interim Report*, Post-16 Education Centre, University of London and Centre for Education and Industry, University of Warwick

Robbins, L (1963) *Higher Education: Report of the Committee*, HMSO, London

Robertson, D (1994) *Choosing to Change: Extending access, choice and mobility in higher education* (the Robertson Report), Higher Education Quality Council, London

Robertson, D (1995) *The Learning Bank: Towards a funding strategy for post-secondary and higher education*, Discussion Paper, Liverpool John Moores University

Robertson, D (1996a) Paying for learning: post-16 education funding must shift from provider to individual, *New Economy*, pp 154–57

Robertson, D (1996b) The Learning Bank and individual learning accounts – emerging policies for funding of relationships in the tertiary learning market, Paper for the CVCP/SRHE Research Seminar, 7 November, John Moores University

Robertson, D (1996c) Policy continuity and progress in the reform of post-compulsory and higher education, in *Boundaries of Adult Learning*, ed R Edwards, R Hanson and P Raggatt, Routledge, London

Robertson, D and Hillman, J (1997a) Individual learning accounts and a Learning Bank, Report No 13, in National Committee of Inquiry into Higher Education, *Higher Education in the Learning Society* (the Dearing Inquiry), NCIHE, London

Robertson, D and Hillman, J (1997b) Widening participation in higher education by students from lower socio-economic groups and students with disabilities, Report No 6, in National Committee of Inquiry into Higher Education, *Higher Education in the Learning Society* (the Dearing Inquiry), Crown Copyright, London

Robinson, P (1996) *Rhetoric and Reality: Britain's new vocational qualifications*, Centre for Economic Performance, London School of Economics

Robinson, P (1998a) Education, training and the youth labour market, in *The State of Working Britain*, ed P Gregg and J Wadsworth, Centre for Economic Performance, London School of Economics

Robinson, P (1998b) Measuring the knowledge economy: employment and qualifications, in *The Knowledge Economy*, ed D Robertson, Macmillan Press, London

Rogers, J and Streeck, W (1994) Productive solidarities, in *Reinventing the Left*, ed D Miliband, IPPR/Polity Press, London

Royal Society (1991) *Beyond GCSE: A report by a working group of the Royal Society's Education Committee*, The Royal Society, London

Royal Society of Arts (1996) *Attitudes to Learning*, MORI State of the Nation Poll Summary Report 1996, RSA, London

Russell, B (1997) Course cut-throats and spies, *Times Educational Supplement*, 12 September

Ryan, P (1998) Is apprenticeship better? A review of the economic evidence, *Journal of Vocational Education and Training*, **50** (2), pp 289–325

Sainsbury plc (1998) *Employment and Training Opportunities for 16–25-year-olds*, Sainsbury, London

Salter, B and Tapper, T (1994) *The State and Higher Education*, The Woburn Press, Ilford

Sargant, N (1996) Learning and 'leisure', in *The Learning Society: Challenges and trends*, ed P Raggatt, R Edwards and N Small, Routledge, London

Sargant, N et al (1997) *The Learning Divide: A study of participation in adult learning in the UK*, NIACE, Leicester

Schagen, S, Johnson, F and Simkin, C (1996) *Sixth Form Options: Post-compulsory education in maintained schools*, NFER, Slough

Schools Curriculum and Assessment Authority and National Council for Vocational Qualifications (SCAA/NCVQ) (1997) *Introducing the National Advanced Diploma*, SCAA, London

Scott, P (1995) *The Meanings of Mass Higher Education*, SRHE and Open University Press, Buckingham

Scott, P (1997) After Dearing, *Scottish Journal of Adult and Continuing Education*, **4** (2), pp 45–55

Scottish Office (1994) *Higher Still: Opportunity for all*, Scottish Office, Edinburgh

Senker, P (1996) Letter from 14 experts on vocational education, *Financial Times*, 17 January

Showstack-Sassoon, A (1998) Some day my prince will come: Gramsci, Blair and modernising projects, *Renewal*, **6** (2), Spring

Smith, Rt Hon A (1998) *Government's Response to the Second Report From the Committee, Session 1997/98: The New Deal*, Education and Employment Committee, House of Commons

Smithers, A (1998) View from here, *The Independent*, 9 April

SOCRATES Project (1998) SOCRATES Making it Work: European Universities and Lifelong Learning Project Briefing Papers, University of Leeds

Soskise, D (1993) Social skills from mass higher education, *Oxford Review of Economic Policy*, **9** (3), Autumn, OUP, Milton Keynes

Spours, K (1993) The reform of qualifications within a divided system, in *The Reform of Post-16 Education and Training in England and Wales*, ed W Richardson, J Woolhouse and D Finegold, Longman, Harlow

Spours, K (1995) *Post-compulsory Education and Training: Statistical trends*, Learning for the Future Working Paper No 7, Post-16 Education Centre, Institute of Education, University of London

Spours, K (1998) *From fragmentation and division towards unification: an analysis of a decade of reform of qualifications from 14+*, PhD thesis, Institute of Education, University of London

Spours, K (1999) Curriculum 14–19: myth – A levels cannot be radically reformed, in *Modern Educational Myths*, Kogan Page, London

Spours, K and Lucas, N (1996) *The Formation of a National Sector of Incorporated Colleges: Developments and contradictions,* Post-16 Education Centre, Working Paper 19, Institute of Education, University of London

Spours, K and Young, M (1996) Dearing and beyond: steps and stages to a unified system, *British Journal of Education and Work,* December

Spours, K et al (1998) *Regulatory and Awarding Bodies and the Process of Unification in England and Scotland*, Working Paper No 5, ESRC Unified Learning Project, University of Edinburgh and Institute of Education, University of London

Stanton, G (1997) Unitization: developing a common language for describing achievement, in *Dearing and Beyond: 14–19 qualifications, frameworks and systems*, ed A Hodgson and K Spours, Kogan Page, London

Steedman, H, Gospel, H and Ryan, P (1998) *Apprenticeship: A strategy for growth*, Centre for Economic Performance, London School of Economics

Steedman, H and Green, A (1996) *Widening Participation in Further Education and Training: A survey of the issues*, Centre for Economic Performance, London

Steedman, H and Green, A (1997) *International Comparison of Skill Supply and Demand*, Centre for Economic Performance, London School of Economics

THES (1999) Ministers act as poor jump ship, *Times Higher Education Supplement*, 29 January

Tight, M (1996) *Key Concepts in Adult Education and Training,* Routledge, London

Trades Union Congress (TUC) (1997) *Investing in Young People: TUC response to the DfEE consultation*, TUC, London

TUC (1998) *New TECs: New parteners*, TUC submission on the DfEE consultation paper, *TECs: Meeting the challenge of the millennium*, TUC, London

Tuckett, A (1997) Foreword, in *The Learning Divide: A study of participation in adult learning in the UK*, ed N Sargant *et al*, NIACE, Leicester

Uden, T (1996) *Widening Participation: Routes to a learning society*, NIACE, Leicester

Unemployment Unit (1998a) Comment, *Working Brief No 90*, Unemployment Unit, London

Unemployment Unit (1998b) Comment, *Working Brief No 100*, Unemployment Unit, London

University and College Admissions Service (UCAS) (1999) Higher Education Applicants, Press Release, 29 January

Unwin, L (1997) Reforming the work-based route: problems and potential for change, in *Dearing and Beyond: 14–19 qualifications, frameworks and systems*, ed A Hodgson and K Spours, Kogan Page, London

Unwin, L and Wellington, J (1995) Reconstructing the work-based route: lessons from the Modern Apprenticeship, *Journal of Vocational Education and Training*, **47** (6), pp 337–52

Vickerstaff, S (1998) The delivery of Modern Apprenticeships: are Training and Enterprise Councils the right mechanism?, *Journal of Vocational Education and Training*, **50** (2), pp 209–24

Weiss, L (1997) The myth of the powerless state, in *New Left Review,* **225,** pp 3–27

Welsh Office (1998) *Learning is for Everyone*, HMSO, London

White, S (1998) Interpreting the 'Third Way': not one road but many, *Renewal*, **6** (2), pp 17–30, Spring

Williamson, B (1996) Repositioning higher education, in *Higher Education and Lifelong Learning*, ed F Coffield, Department of Education, University of Newcastle upon Tyne

Wilson, P (1993) Developing a post-16 CAT framework: the technical specifications, in *Discussing Credit: A collection of occasional papers relating to the FEU proposal for a post-16 credit accumulation and transfer framework*, FEU, London

Wolf, A (1992) *An Assessment-driven System: Education and training in England and Wales*, Institute of Education, University of London

Young, M and Spours, K (1998) 14–19 education legacy, opportunities and challenges, *Oxford Review of Education*, **24** (1), pp 83–97

Young, M *et al* (1998) *The Process of Unification: The case of Wales,* ESRC Unified Learning Project, Paper 9, University of Edinburgh and Institute of Education, University of London

Youthaid, Barnados and The Children's Society (1997) *New Deal – Fair Deal? Experiences of black young people in the labour market*, Youthaid, London

Index

Index

Visit Kogan Page on-line

Comprehensive information on
Kogan Page titles

Features include

- complete catalogue listings,
  including book reviews and
  descriptions

- special monthly promotions

- information on NEW titles and
  BESTSELLING titles

- a secure shopping basket facility
  for on-line ordering

PLUS everything you need to know
about KOGAN PAGE

http://www.kogan-page.co.uk